I CAN TELL GOD

Anything

Living Prayer

I CAN TELL GOD

Anything

Living Prayer

JEAN MAALOUF

SHEED & WARD

Franklin, Wisconsin

As an apostolate of the Priests of the Sacred Heart, a Catholic religious congregation, the mission of Sheed & Ward is to publish books of contemporary impact and enduring merit in Catholic Christian thought and action. The books published, however, reflect the opinions of their authors and are not meant to represent the official position of the Priests of the Sacred Heart.

2000

SHEED & WARD
7373 South Lovers Lane Road
Franklin, Wisconsin 53132
1-800-266-5564

Printed in the United States of America

Cover and interior design by Robin Booth
Author photo by Heidi Johnson

Scripture quotations are from the New Revised Standard Version of the Bible, copyright 1989 by the Division of Christian Education of the National Council of the Churches of Christ in the USA. Used by permission. All rights reserved.

Part II of this work is based on material that was previously published in *The Catechist's Connection*.

Library of Congress Cataloging-in-Publication Data
Maalouf, Jean.
  I can tell God anything : living prayer / Jean Maalouf.
     p. cm.
  ISBN 1-58051-071-X (alk. paper)
  Prayers. 2. Prayer—Catholic Church. I. Title
BV229 .M22 2000
242' .802—dc21   99-055493

CONTENTS

DEDICATION

To my parents and all my loved ones,
here and in eternity,
and to all those who recognize God
in anyone,
through anything,
in anyplace,
at anytime.

Pray without ceasing.

—1 THESSALONIANS 5:17

---

*Whether you eat or drink, or whatever you do,
do everything for the glory of God.*

—1 CORINTHIANS 10:31

$\mathcal{I}$NTRODUCTION

P<small>RAYER IS MORE</small> than the words we say or the rituals we perform. Prayer is an attitude of living and a state of being and loving. This is why one can "pray without ceasing" (1 Thessalonians 5:17).

There are many books written on prayer from which one can learn of the theology of prayer, the ways of prayer, the history of prayer, the healing power of prayer, the necessity and usefulness of prayer, etc. Most of these books are excellent treatises of prayer, from their particular points of view. In this book, I do not intend to repeat what has already been said about prayer many times throughout history.

Although the theoretical part with reference to Scripture, theology, philosophy, psychology, spirituality, and mysticism is important, the main objective of this book is to show how we can and must "pray without ceasing" and become living prayer. This means that we will have to involve our whole person in prayer, and involve prayer in all that we do at every moment of life, in every place.

Isn't it about time we heal that ancient division of spirit-matter that greatly distorts our concepts of prayer and the God to whom we pray? Prayer is not mere "thinking about" God, and being Christian is not a matter of having a better knowledge of God. Rather, union with God comes through love rather than knowledge, for:

> *"They who have my commandments and keep*
> *them are those who love me; and those who love*
> *me will be loved by my Father, and I will love*
> *them and reveal myself to them"* (John 14:21).

Accepting the Lord, then, is not a conceptual concord, acquiescence, or ascent; rather, it is a loving acceptance of Jesus Christ himself. This means that the emotional part of the person who is praying has its own importance and priority among the ingredients that make a fervent prayer. For this reason, I chose to write these spontaneous prayers that welled up from the very core of my being. In these prayers, I tell God all I have in my mind and heart—and then I reflect on what I've told him. God knows what is going on in the secret of our secrets, of course, but he loves to hear it directly from our own hearts and minds. In the end, only love counts—not rationalization and not even perfect speculations. "Sir," the woman said, "give me this water, so that I may never be thirsty or have to keep coming here to draw water" (John 4:15).

Although traditional methodology—of putting the definitions and principles first, then applying life to these definitions and principles—has merit, I chose not to use it. I just pray—then I philosophize about prayer. In that way, *essence* will make more sense, for it is known through *existence*. This is what I would like to call an existential, incarnational, lifelong prayer.

This book will show that prayer is not necessarily a hunger for immediate results, a sign of infantilism and cowardice, or some kind of religious rescue as a last resort in time of turmoil. It is not an eloquent speech to God intended to convince him of something, to change his mind about something, or to manipulate him to intervene at once in some critical situation or because we do not have time to take care of the situation ourselves. Prayer is not an escape from a difficult problem, a medical prescription that has the power to work like a drug, or a psychological trick to convince ourselves that everything is or will be fine. Prayer is not a part-time job that we skillfully perform when we need to change God's mind about something. No! Prayer—and the object of this book—is an entering into the constant practice of the presence and involvement of a loving God within us and in our lives at all times and in all places.

God, through prayer, does not change. Rather, we change through prayer. Prayer is our way of experiencing God through our connectedness with the concrete situations in our lives, not just through those images and concepts that we usually have a tendency to use. In prayer, we do not simply *think* about God; rather, we *live* God, and we invite God to *live within* us. Prayer is a theological grace that transforms our being here on earth. It is the Holy Spirit working in our being through our every breath.

Prayer, then, is not what we do for God, but rather what the Spirit does in us, for us, and through us. The best prayer is when we open our hearts to God and let him pray within us.

Then, whatever we do becomes a living prayer. Prayer is our way of letting God do his work in us and through us. Let us not interfere. Let us allow God space and time. Let us allow God to be the action. Without his divine and generous grace, we are unable to make one single act of faith, hope, charity, and prayer. Prayer includes all our concerns, worries, joys, works, thoughts, words, feelings, choices, and actions. All our life should be prayer. With God's help, we can "pray without ceasing." We can be "living prayer." We can become saints. We can achieve holiness—no matter what we do for a living or where we are in life.

Holiness is not the profession of only the pious priests, bishops, monks, and cloistered nuns who chant the Divine Office in the wee hours of the morning. The Second Vatican Council said that all the faithful of Christ are to pursue holiness. From where we are—from within our own individual situations in life—we can love God with our whole heart and soul and mind, and our neighbor as ourselves. Authentic holiness is tested by this direct relationship with God and with others—no matter who they are—and by our capacity to allow God to transform our entire lives into living prayer. The index of holiness is in the experience of the presence of God, whom we do not see, and the loving of others, whom we do see (see 1 John 4:20). The way we treat others, much more than some ruthless self-denial, is the barometer that truly measures the genuineness of our union with God and our continuous state of living prayer—our true holiness. Our love of God ought to be expressed concretely, every day, in the here and now.

Oh, how many times we practice our religion, but in hypocrisy. We give to the poor, but we don't want to meet them. We go to church and greet the people we can't stand, nod approvingly at the homilies that bore us, confess sins we did not commit, and forget the sins we really did commit. We repeat our "churchy" prayers again and again, even though we might not be paying attention to the One who is supposed to be listening—and we pretend to be better persons for having said all these prayers. Shouldn't we be honest at least with God, who knows all our inner secrets anyway? Shouldn't we admit that, even if we seem over-developed outwardly, we might be under-developed inwardly? Let us not pretend! Rather, let us live our love of God fully. Let us live our prayers daily and concretely. Let us "get real" in living holiness.

The prayers and confessions that constitute the first section of this book are realistic, i.e., real, and existential. They are not the type of cliché prayers one usually repeats, and they are not fiction. Rather, they are living prayers. They happened in time and place, and they describe, intimately and in direct language, spiritual journeys with God. Most of them describe my own personal experiences, although a few describe the experiences of others. All of them are just like each one of us—no more, no less. They reflect our contradictions and confusions, as well as our determination to focus on God. They are genuine.

God wants us to be true. God wants us to speak boldly to him in every possible manner: joyfully, gratefully, friendlily, needfully, patiently, nervously, perseveringly, faithfully, desperately, spontaneously, thoughtfully, in tears, in silence, with words—even in anger and unbelief. No time, no place, no circumstance, no mood, no ideology, can keep us apart from God. He does not censure our prayers. Rather, anything we ask in God's name, he will do (see John 14:14). Do you hear this? *Anything!* God knows we live in a complicated world. He knows our weaknesses and troubles, our successes and failures. He knows we are growing. He knows everything and he wants to share in it all. We allow this through prayer.

Prayer is not a ritual; rather, it is the response to a loving relationship with a loving God. There is no better prayer than the feeling of being aware of God in us and telling him that which we would tell no one else. This is how God likes us to be—as fully human as possible. This is how we reach out to one another; this is how we become more universal. Paradoxically, the more human we are, the more holy and divine we become. To live fully our humaneness is an essential part of our prayerful life. To be fully human and fully divine is what the mystery of the Incarnation has revealed we should be—for Jesus was both.

The reflections on prayer that constitute the second section of this book are intended to shed light, using concrete examples, on what prayer is, why we pray, how we pray, who the God is to whom we pray, what kind of prayer we usually pray, etc. Some of these reflections are based on material that appeared in *The Catechist's Connection* under the title "How We Pray."

"Unceasing prayer" and "living prayer": This is what our lives are meant to be. Being in love with the Lord in a prayer relationship must be our ultimate goal in life. Lord, "give me that water! Then I will never be thirsty again."

Please pray with me for both of us today and always, for real prayer heals the soul, mind, heart, and body. Prayer provides us with joy and the inner sense of God's peace. It helps us to bring meaning to our suffering and our losses, thus to give ultimate meaning to our lives. "Give me that water!"

PART ONE

I Can Tell God
Anything

LORD,

Christmas is an amazing time! Wherever we go—to the store, the post office, the bank, the mall, anywhere—we find ourselves *waiting*. We seem to rush everywhere, yet everywhere we go, we wait—we wait to send a card or buy a gift; we wait in line, in traffic, and in the crowd. Yet, we don't seem to be bothered with all this—when at other times, we might become nervous and frazzled. In fact, we rather like the joy of it. It's Christmas! At Christmas, we like the crowd, the rush, the snow and ice, the light and darkness, the trees, the songs, the waiting—everything. After all, this is part of the Christmas spirit. One's spirit changes when Christmas is in the air.

This year, however, after I sent my cards and purchased my gifts, I said: "What about me?" I looked around for my gift, one just for me. I checked every store in the area, and at a distance—a larger town where it took me two hours just to find a small space to park my compact car. Nowhere did I find what I was looking for. No one carried what I wanted. What I was looking for was not on display anywhere.

I was looking for "to live without fear"—and money cannot buy this kind of thing.

Dear Lord,

Somehow I feel that I live my life in fear, and I don't know exactly why. Is it because of the way I grew up, the way I was educated and learned to handle things? Is it because of my culture, society, and the groups I belong to? Is it how the human condition is supposed to be? The fact is, I often live in fear; sometimes I even tremble.

I fear to fail and I fear to succeed.

I fear not to be loved and I fear to be loved.

I fear men and women who intimidate me and I fear those who are my friends.

I fear losing my job and not being able to perform what I am supposed to do, and I fear staying in the same job forever.

I fear growing old alone and I fear spending the rest of my life with my soul mate.

I fear withdrawing in solitude and I fear belonging to a community.

I fear going broke, being disrespected and avoided, and I fear being successful and rich, honored and bombarded by reporters.

I fear being sick, not being able to take care of myself and no longer having the choice to go wherever I want, and I fear the one who can take care of me when I can no longer decide for myself.

I fear controlling others and I fear being controlled.

Above all I fear my belief system that keeps torturing me with thoughts such as: "You should be the best. You have to work hard. You have to please people. You must be the author everyone is waiting for. You must obey God in everything"— etc., etc.

Yes, I must obey God. I do and I don't.

Lord, I am trying my best—you know that, don't you?

My Christmas Gift

But on the question of fear, I fail to follow your teachings. You said:

> *"I tell you, do not worry about your life, what you will eat or what you will drink, or about your body, what you will wear. Is not life more than food, and the body more than clothing? Look at the birds of the air; they neither sow nor reap nor gather into barns, and yet your heavenly Father feeds them. Are you not of more value than they? And can any of you by worrying add a single hour to your span of life? And why do you worry about clothing? Consider the lilies of the field, how they grow; they neither toil nor spin, yet I tell you, even Solomon in all his glory was not clothed like one of these. But if God so clothes the grass of the field, which is alive today and tomorrow is thrown into the oven, will he not much more clothe you—you of little faith? Therefore do not worry, saying, 'What will we eat?' or 'What will we drink?' or 'What will we wear?' For it is the Gentiles who strive for all these things; and indeed your heavenly Father knows that you need all these things. But strive first for the kingdom of God and his righteousness, and all these things will be given to you as well. So do not worry about tomorrow, for tomorrow will bring worries of its own. Today's trouble is enough for today"* (Matthew 6:25–34).

My Christmas Gift

You also said: "It is I; do not be afraid" (Matthew 14:27) and "Get up and do not be afraid" (Matthew 17:7).

I fail to obey you here, Lord—yet I must obey you. Please, Lord, help me to start at once, right here.

So my Christmas gift this year is called "trust." From now on, I am going to trust you and be afraid no longer. You said so—and I believe you. I believe in you. I take you at your word, literally, seriously. I count on you. You are with me. I am afraid no more.

What a relief!

What a Christmas gift! In fact, this gift is so precious that even the largest store in the world cannot afford to display it on its shelves. It is much bigger than any store, and much more precious.

It is so big that it took all the mystery of your Incarnation to make it available to the world. The manger did not scare you, neither did the cross. You trusted.

Lord, give me the gift of counting on you, trusting you, starting to live without fear.

Also, I ask you to help me share this most beautiful gift with others, for I know that the more I share it with others, the greater and more beautiful it becomes.

Thank you, Lord, for revealing to me the mystery of trust. Amen.

✛

LORD,

I am not satisfied with the prayers I pray on Sunday.
I go to the service and I do what I am supposed to do, but
there is something missing.

There must be more to the spiritual life than going to
church on Sunday.

Sunday prayer is fine, but it is like a part-time job—and
I want a full-time job.

Paul, your apostle, says that we should "pray without
ceasing," and this makes more sense to me. But how, dear
Lord, how to do this?

My solution is this: I am going to eat, drink, go to
work, come home, go to bed, and wake up in the morning
while I am thinking of you and how you would do things. I
am going to become like a little child and look at things with
wonder. I am going to play more; I am going to do all things
playfully. I am going to enjoy seeing the rich color of a rose,
hearing the wind between the pines, tasting a yellow apple
with delight, and touching the soft fur on my dog's head.

Today I am not going to solve world problems—or even
my own. What I am going to do today, however, is pick up
this telephone and reach out to that ninety-year-old man,
who is tragically alone, and provide him with warmth, concern, and love. Then I am going to take a hot dish to a poor
woman with two babies. Then I am going to make an extra
effort to communicate your love to whomever I meet today,
especially my students. This is what I am going to do today.

The needs of these people you put on my way are more real than the visions I am working on—as important as they may be—and it will probably be more pleasing to you, Lord, if I help them any way I can. Your gospel says that on the day of judgment you will ask me whether or not I loved, not whether or not I created a beautiful system of world justice.

Let the goal of my prayer, then, be love, not excellence in performance.

Also, I am going to pay attention to everything I do and explore the hidden dimensions behind the obvious. In this loaf of bread in front of me, I am going to see the grain of wheat, the earth where it was planted, the sun shining upon it, the rain quenching its thirst, the air enveloping the kernel, the laborer in the harvest, the baker in the bakery, the distributor in the car—and you, dear Lord, the origin of all this. I am going to see you in the hearts of people who eat this bread.

Let my prayer be an expression of my gratitude to you.

I want to be grateful to you forever.

I want to pray without ceasing.

I want to be a living prayer.

LORD,

I am trying to hear you. Please help me to detect exactly what your plan is for me—and then help me to not get in your way.

I concede that, at the deepest level of my being, your call rather frees me. In fact, it enables me to focus on what really matters: *you.* To love you with my whole heart, mind, and soul is the very reason for my living. This is my special calling.

But I cannot afford to go it alone—I really can't. I need your support for my commitment to you.

Our culture at the present time does not help in this. What once was generally accepted as values—in institutions like governments and churches, marriage and family life, vows and monastic life, to mention just a few—are becoming almost another page in the history of humankind. It seems so, at least, according to the perceptions we used to have.

If it is to last, commitment needs something greater to count on. By itself, a once dearly held commitment becomes impossible to sustain unless your grace makes it hold. After all, we are continuously changing creatures—physically, psychologically, and spiritually.

To make a commitment is a mysterious faith process. To alter a commitment, once made in good faith, requires trust in life and in you. There are so many ways to think, feel, and be in life. Only the call I hear from you, dear Lord, stays the same: to love you and love my neighbor as myself. But, how—here and now, with whom, in what place and context—should this love be materialized?

Lord,

You want me to be what I am, but what I am is what you want me to be. I want to be faithful to this truth. I want to keep my choices grounded in my deepest calling, the calling that focuses on my willingness and determination to love you no matter what the circumstances are and how it is expressed— and no matter the cost.

Lord,

Help me to answer your call properly, the best I can, in the way you choose for me.

No matter how your call is expressed in me, gently or even explosively, help me to respond to it in daily fidelity and obedient love. Your call is the truth of my own life. I want to be faithful to that call—totally. Don't let me get in the way of your plans for me. Make a difference in my own life, so that through me, a difference will be made around me.

Lord,

Our age today needs saints—more than it needs advanced technologies, brilliant scientists, canny politicians, perfect athletes, and so many other things people consider crucially important. Make me one of the saints that our age needs today.

Our age needs people of substance, integrity, truth, and great goodness. Make me one of these people our age desperately needs today.

Isn't this deep longing for you and your ways, dear Lord, what my special calling is truly about?

Lord, make of my life a continuous commitment to your call.

Amen.

The Call

LORD,

Very soon I am going to hit the road. Please help me to be totally awake, alert, careful, patient, courteous, and polite. I want to be a good driver.

Remind me, Lord, of my responsibilities: toward others, myself, my family. Remind me of my limitations as well.

Keep the road clear from drunk drivers and those who take drugs, as well as those who do not appreciate the value of life.

Inspire me to make the right decisions and to have the appropriate and quick reflexes to react toward unexpected circumstances. Inspire others to do the same.

Above all, Lord, let me always be in your presence. Let me live under your protection. Help others to be aware and do the same.

Amen.

LORD,

Thank you for the sun, the moon, the birds, the flowers, the fresh air, and the beautiful friends you have blessed me with.

Thank you for opening my eyes to see you in everyone, to hear you in every sound, to feel you in every thing.

Life is so beautiful—and so meaningful—when it is filled with you. Grant me that feeling of never being in despair in any situation—never, never.

To the disciples who had worked in vain all night long, you said: "Cast the net to the right side of the boat" (John 21:6). When they did, they couldn't even pull the net because it was so full of fish.

Trust is miraculous.

All my calculations, speculations, and expectations are in vain—even wrong. Only when I cast my net where you tell me to—only when I surrender to you—do things come right. Unexpectedly. Spontaneously. Mysteriously. Your way.

Lord, you are full of surprises.

Thank you for blessing me with your messengers in my journey through life.

Thank you for putting along my way two special messengers who, in various manners, pointed out to me what you really wanted from me.

"Follow the call where it takes you," he said. "It is he again," she said. "It is not from me; it is through me," and "Don't forget to give your smile away."

What a sensitivity! What a wisdom! What a generosity of spirit!

Now I know that your gospel is possible, actual, and realistic.

Another Incarnation.

I do see it. It is possible. It is real.

Thank you for letting me read your words not in a book this time, but through life.

Right from the start, they sensed my inner calling and helped me in many ways to make my American dream—to make a contribution for a better world—come true.

Please, Lord, protect them and their loved ones. Grant them long life and the health and prosperity they certainly deserve. Find solutions for all the problems they might have in life. Be always their solution.

Be with them all the time—day and night. Also, be with all the beautiful friends they have introduced me to.

Let the flames of their candles light the other candles that are still thirsty for their light—your flame.

And don't allow me to forget the help they are offering to me: their support, their assistance, their presence, their insights, their steady encouragement, their prompt readiness for service, their anxious concern—your Good News!

Thank you, Lord, for all your messengers, especially for these. You—only you—know how grateful I am for them. And you—only you—know how to reward them. For any reward, besides you, is too little.

Amen.

✛

LORD,

Teach me your ways of innocence, poverty in spirit, vulnerability, honesty, and total surrender.

I know that you are at the door, for I hear you knocking. But I am busy doing so many things.

I am so preoccupied with how to reach you, how to know you, and how to live your word—so busy that I don't answer you.

I am so worried about what to read, what to write, what to say, what to do, and what to produce. Yet, you are still knocking.

I am so concerned with my achievements, successes, and the quality of my relationships, that I have not yet answered the door.

Enter, Lord. Please enter.

Give me a growing desire to live as if you are the only Lord of my life, for you are the Lord of my life.

Make me honest, direct, and poor in spirit. Help me to understand that all my worries, concerns, and preoccupations—even for you—are not, in fact, *you*.

Let me feel that knowing you is not to acquire more knowledge of you but to drop all these games and simply love you—freely and boldly.

The way to you is not just thinking of you. Rather, it is in peeling off all those layers of mere talking about you and of recounting only good things about you. In getting rid of my many illusions and rationalizations, I can more easily reach your truths—and you.

The way to you is the way of emptiness—emptiness from things and from the concept of the remote creator and abstract God—so that you can act directly in my soul. The way to you is the way of innocence, poverty in spirit, vulnerability, honesty, and total surrender.

Please Lord,

Help me to destroy all the barriers I've carefully built to prevent you from doing what you would like to do with me.

Help me to clean my house from all things that I have stored there. I know that the more I can throw away the things from my life, the more space I make available just for you.

Make from my house your home.

Amen.

Make from My House Your Home

LORD,

We seem to be crazy about weather news. We want to know what the weather is going to be like today, then we want to know what it will be like tomorrow, next week, and even the week after that. We even have special television channels that give us a continuous report about the weather, everywhere, any time.

Spring comes and goes, summer comes and goes, autumn comes and goes, and winter comes and goes—almost the same way every year. We have no control over how seasons come and go.

However, we can control the "weather" feelings within us, which we rarely do. We can control our thoughts, emotions, and attitudes toward others. Why don't we do it?

We can remove unhealthy negative belief systems and create "favorable conditions" for healthy individuals and a healthy planet. Why don't we do it?

We can stop complaining about a hot summer and a cold winter. We can take care of the air we breathe, the water we drink, and the trees we touch. Why don't we do it?

We can withdraw to some little solitude, from time to time, and blow out the toxins in the air we've breathed in from our industrial, so-called civilized society. We can diffuse our negative thoughts toward others. Why don't we do it?

We can think about how miraculous and interesting our lives are. They really are as intriguing—if not more so—than the moon and the stars. Why don't we realize this?

We can listen to our hearts. We can pay attention to all that we come into contact with. According to their original designs, then, we can enjoy them more fully, more effectively, more enthusiastically, and more peacefully. Why don't we do this?

We can invite you into our lives, into who we are and what we happen to be doing. Why don't we do it?

We can listen more, love more, care more, and be more. Why don't we do it?

We can create the "right climate" within us, one that affects the climate without. Then every morning, we can go outside and greet the beginning of the day—no matter what the weather is—by just enjoying it and thanking you for another beautiful and generous morning. Why don't we just do this?

Lord,

Help us to see you where you are, not in some abstract concept but in all things. Help us to identify with you, for the more we identify with you, the more we become ourselves.

Help us to live prayerfully in all kinds of weather, clear and stormy, within and without.

Amen.

✛

LORD,

Except for the falling snow, the high wind, and the thickening ice, almost everything else had stopped. The blizzard of January 8, 1996, kept everyone home. The United States superpower couldn't do anything about it, and the greater New York area became like a far-away mountain village.

The city, however, was beautiful under the white blanket and, somehow, it rediscovered its original charm. For that one day an immaculate snow covered the entire dirty side of our civilization. And on that day no pollution of any kind was mentioned. There was no violence, no indifference, no selfishness—nothing but snow.

People changed on that day. They talked to one another, smiled at one another, helped one another. They provided shelter for one another and enjoyed the taste of togetherness. They became humane again. They became normal people on that snow-white day.

Although it was a big mess that paralyzed the city, Lord, and it was an even bigger mess to clean up the streets afterwards, a blizzard like that reminds us of the limitations of our so-called superpowerness, the innocence of our original humanness and our dependence on you.

Lord,

Let the blizzard blow away the dark side of our civilization, our pursuits of a fictitious happiness, our diversions, our masks, our lies, and our suspicious lifestyles. And let the white snow, before it melts, open our eyes and hearts and souls to see the innocence of our original humanness that we might live it perfectly.

    Amen.

LORD,

I live in a town where winter is often snowy and icy. For weeks my town can be white and my windows covered by two-foot icicles.

Snow gives charm to this town, especially at Christmas. This year, the mixture of snow, cold, lights, and candles lit in bags all over the center of town was marvelous.

But snow and ice can be annoying, too.

There is a man, and several others like him, who loves to keep the town going. This man, a mechanic, repairs all kinds of trucks. He himself has a good truck. As soon as snow starts to fall, he attaches a plow to his truck and starts to clean the roads, early—very early—in the morning, while the rest of us are still in bed, and in the morning everyone goes to work on time.

This man, in his own way, keeps the social structures going. He loves it—and people love him.

Lord,

Give the necessary energy to this man to continue to do the work he does. And let him know that his work is a real ministry. Plowing the snow is a way to follow you. His work contributes to the smooth running of public life—and thus, he contributes to your work in the world. He opens the roads to others and helps them keep going.

Give that same energy to other workers: manufacturers, bakers, cooks, food production workers, secretaries, bosses, professionals, sweepers, masons, taxi drivers, all communications workers, etc. All of them, in their own way, are co-creators with you in the daily world, the way you want it to be.

When all these people know what they are doing and why, and when you are truly present in them, they are certainly following you. Let us understand, dear Lord, that we can follow you without necessarily aping you. You did not do all these jobs—and, at times, these jobs can be boring, unrewarding, and dissatisfying. But still we can imagine how you would have done this or that job if you had to. We can follow you through our being, our attitudes, our thoughts, our feelings, our ideas, and our behavior. For it is not *what* we do that is important, but the *way* we do it—and you are the Way. Being Christian at work means bringing your presence into the world. Wherever Christians are, you are present—through bishops, nuns, priests, professors, plumbers, farmers, lawyers, mechanics, salespersons, cashiers, everyone.

All that we do, touch, sense, drink, eat, walk on, and play with can and should be the wellsprings of our own spirituality. These actions can and should be real prayers. The Sunday prayer is necessary, and it is a good start. But prayer should include the whole of life throughout the week—week after week. This is what I am trying to do, dear Lord.

Lord, make my dreams of secular sanctity a concrete reality. Let whatever I do become a ministry to give glory to you, my Lord and my God.

Amen.

✛

The Ministry of Plowing

LORD,

When I say, "Thy will be done—not my will, but thine," I get the feeling that what I say is somehow a lie. It translates a profound hypocrisy.

Although "Thy will be done" has the appearance of being a true prayer—maybe the truest—it does not seem sincere and, somehow, it does not express an act of faith. Rather, it often translates an attitude of inertia, perhaps of cowardice and especially convenience. It is like saying, "I am not going to change God's mind, so it is better to align my self with God because whatever happens is, in fact, his will and he does whatever he has in mind anyway."

"Thy will be done" is a beautiful prayer, but it can be a hidden sin as well. If I mean that nothing can be done because you are going to do whatever you want to do, I am imagining that you are a kind of despot, a tyrant, who does not tolerate others' ideas. And behind this formula, I hide my belief that you are, in fact, *not* good, *not* Father, *not* friend, *not* Love. What a sin!

Dear Lord, I don't mean to be rude, but I want to say exactly what is in my mind and heart. If we are friends, we should be able to be together with open minds and open hearts—and aren't we good friends?

The other thing I want to tell you, while we are on this subject, is that I sometimes have a tendency to count on you too much. This is good, and there is usually nothing wrong with it. But the bad part is that sometimes I do things with the intention of not wanting to be held accountable—and I become indifferent and irresponsible. So my full counting on you becomes a "religious exit" for my laziness and passivity, an escape for not being in charge—along with you—of my own life.

Dear Lord, more than ever, I am going to continue saying, "Thy will be done." But I am not going to put all my confidence in this formula, even if it is from your Scripture. I know that even Satan, in this sense, can pray and repeat the gospel more than any of your closest friends.

From now on I am going to say "Thy will be done" with awareness, lucidity, and resolution—and at the same time I am going to work as hard as I can to do what I am asking for. Do not misunderstand me, dear Lord. I want to surrender to you completely. But you don't want me to have this kind of resignation and passive attitude, do you? Why have you given me intelligence, will, courage, and the energy for creating things if you don't want me to use them?

As I see it, you take care of the creation of your hands—but you don't send food to the house through the chimney. Rather, you provide a living through the things you give us, much as you provide food for the birds through the wings you give them.

Dear Lord, give me the grace to count on you through the wings you have given me.

Amen.

✛

LORD,

Today, I do not feel okay.

I feel somehow discouraged, baffled, bewildered.

I am worried, very worried.

I am worried about my past, for not having done what I dreamed. I am worried about the present and the future, for I am not sure of making the right decisions and doing the right things.

I am worried about being able—or not being able—to make it.

I am worried about my health, my income, my house, my car, my job, my family, my friends. I am worried about getting old—and even about the weather.

Sometimes I feel as though I'm paralyzed and cannot act.

Lord, this is a terrible feeling. I am supposed to let it go out of my system. Without counting the catastrophic consequences from the mental and the spiritual point of view, this feeling is dangerous. Worrying, after all, can have serious results at the physical level as well. Studies have shown that worrying can cause ulcers, high blood pressure, heart ailments, asthma, colitis, arthritis, poor eyesight, skin diseases—to mention just a few of the side effects. Any one of them is enough to make me want to get rid of my worries as quickly as I can.

So I have to get rid of my worries.

But how to do that, dear Lord? How? What is the solution?

The studies I've read recommend building physical and mental barriers to worries. These studies emphasize the importance of sufficient sleep, nourishing food, fresh air, and physical activities. They also emphasize positive and active thinking. They suggest that I discard problems I can do nothing about and learn to accept what I cannot change. The studies also tell me to learn from children. When children learn to ride a bicycle, for example, they may make a lot of mistakes, but they don't worry about them. They simply try again. They correct the mistakes they've made and, eventually, they learn how to ride a bicycle. Babies learn to walk by falling many times; they seem to naturally turn their mistakes into learning assets.

The studies also recommend balancing my worries with my blessings (your blessings to me are many, and I sometimes forget about them), perspectives, and visions (I also have them and forget about them). They also suggest that I pray. Praying, they say, is the one thing you can do when you can't do anything else. It gives you the same feeling you get when you call the doctor—the sense that help is on the way.

So I am going to try this. Without neglecting the other advice the studies offer, I have decided to take you, dear Lord, as my partner. I know that I can't offer you much as your partner, so this partnership seems unfair to you. But please join me. Help me to be the best I can be. Then you would accept me, at least for my good intention and great efforts. I do not know exactly how you can help me, Lord, but I want your help. I now put myself, my family, my job, my past, my future, my worries, into your hands, and I will do whatever you say. You gave me this day and all that I have.

Do Not Worry about Your Worries

They are my blessings and I am glad to have them. Thank you. I have made some mistakes in the past when I did not follow your advice. Please forgive me. On the other hand, I had some victories when I did followed your guidance. I am proud of those victories, for you recommended: "Let your light shine before others, so that they may see your good works and give glory to your Father in heaven" (Matthew 5:16). Plus, from now on, I am going to follow the advice of your friend, Paul: "This one thing I do: forgetting what lies behind and straining forward to what lies ahead, I press on toward the goal for the prize of the heavenly call of God in Christ Jesus" (Philippians 3:13-14). It worked for Paul. It will work for me as well.

So I am no longer going to worry about my worries. I count completely and totally upon you.

Amen.

LORD,

I heard the priest say that you love children. Thank you for loving me.

Now I know you have a special preference for those who know how to play. You must like the little ones, those who are simple, direct, honest, innocent, and without too many worries.

You must have a great sense of humor.

You must also have a sharp taste for wonder, imagination, and dreams. Don't you?

I want to "thank you for this day," as Mom would say.

I played a lot today. I lost twice and I won five times. Not bad. Can't you always be part of our team so that we will never lose?

My friends love me and I love them. Thank you for giving me these friends. Thank you for being the dearest one among them.

Also, thank you for giving me my feet so that I can walk and run under the tree that I love so much. Thank you for giving me my hands so that I can pick the beautiful violets. Thank you for giving me my nose so that I can smell their sweet fragrance. Thank you for giving me my eyes so that I can admire their beauty. Thank you for letting me sense, feel, think, talk, laugh, enjoy, and be happy.

Thank you for Mom and Dad, for my sister and brother, and for Grandpa and Grandma. I love them all, even if my brother gives me a hard time sometimes.

Thank you for being my best friend.
Thank you for the miracle of love.
Thank you for the miracle of each new day.
Amen.

LORD,

Please help me to be holy.

No, not necessarily by being a hermit in a cave or an ascetic living in some secluded sacred place. The hermit and the ascetic have their legitimate place in holiness and their reasons for withdrawing from the world, for denying themselves and the world, and for living for spiritual things only. This is their way to you.

I don't think, Lord, that their way is my way, however. Are you going to ask me one day why I didn't become like one of the great Desert Fathers? Are you going to ask me whether or not I abstained from the goods of the world instead of enjoying them properly? Are you going to ask me whether or not I became as perfect as the goody-goody perfectionists who never do anything wrong? Probably not. You will most likely ask me why I didn't become me. So help me to become myself, my true self, where I am, with what I am doing.

You are not going to ask me how much money I have in the bank, but whether or not I helped others in any way I could. So help me to help others, Lord, in loving ways.

You are not going to ask me whether or not I cursed the world you created and the life you gave me, but what I did with the world and with my life. So help me to love the world and life with passionate service. Then I will contribute to changing the world by pulling it closer to you.

You are not going to ask me whether or not I loved you in the abstract, as a beautiful and coherent concept and as an invisible Mighty Being, but whether or not I loved my spouse, my children, my parents, my neighbors, the stranger in need, the prisoner, the sick, the lonely—everyone. So help me to love and love and love, even—maybe especially—the clearly imperfect humans around me.

You are not going to ask me how many religious services I skillfully performed or how many Divine Offices I said, for you recommended that I leave the temple and be reconciled with my brother and sister before I present my offerings at the altar. So help me to be reconciled with my brother and sister, to practice forgiveness by learning what it means to be "loved anyway."

You are not going to ask me whether or not I gave up all human pleasures and lived just for the spirit, for you enjoyed being with your friends; you enjoyed having parties, laughing, crying, sharing feelings, and being human. So help me, Lord, to be as human as I possibly can.

You are not going to ask me how many times I said "Lord, Lord," or how intense my feelings for serenity and good will were, for you recommended: "Not everyone who says to me, 'Lord, Lord,' will enter the kingdom of heaven, but only the one who does the will of my Father in heaven" (Matthew 7:21). So help me to live up to your will, to live what I "preach," and to accommodate my ethics and my behavior to my good will, serenity, and prayers. Help me, Lord, to understand that religion is for living faith not just for reading or talking about doing great things.

Holiness: A Lifestyle

You are not going to ask me how many degrees I have or whether I can recite by heart Scripture verses to defend you before an adversary, for you recommended that our righteousness should surpass that of the scribes and Pharisees (see Matthew 5:19). You recommended that I be simple, spontaneous, and innocent, like "little children," otherwise I cannot enter the kingdom of God. So help me to be like a little child.

You are not going to ask me whether or not I was perfect—thank God—infallible and without sin, for only *you* are infallible, and life is infallible because you are at work within it. So let me feel you in life, touch you, see you, hear you, taste you, "live" you. Let the waters of life bring me to the port of sanctity. Let me be loyal to life, for life is divine, the highest degree of sanctity. You are "the way, and the truth, and the life" (John 14:5). And since you are also the goal of all life, let me bring all my vital forces and the vital forces of the entire universe to you. Let me live fully, so fully that I can reach that energy that holds things together, the sap of the universe, the ground of our being: divine love.

Lord,

Make me holy. Make me love life and live life fully, for it is life—you—who shows others the way by living the truth. Let not the reasonable, philosophical, and orthodox theological answers be the answers to my life; rather, let *you* be the answer to my life. If the world is not yet holy, it is because I am not yet holy.

Lord,

Make me holy by making me fully alive, the way you are. Amen.

LORD,

Okay, I learned my lesson this time. You put me in the simple atmosphere of simple workers to learn to be simple.

Wasn't this your purpose, after all?

Now I know!

Thirty years you lived unknown, unseen, unnoticed, hidden, and simple in your world.

You were not an important personality in your society, yet you did what the most powerful people failed to do.

You were not a doctor of anything, yet you taught even in the synagogues, proclaiming the Good News.

You were not a scholar, yet doctors, rabbis, and teachers came to learn from you.

You did not have the most powerful army in the world, yet you changed the world with fishermen and other ordinary people.

You did not have a house, a car, a position, a famous name, or any "connections"—not even insurance—yet you survived well until the time we couldn't stand your love and words any longer and we nailed you on the cross.

What was your secret, dear Lord? What was your secret?

Why is your simplicity so magnetic, so intriguing, so mysteriously sophisticated, so loving?

Is this what you meant when you said: "I am the way, and the truth, and the life" (John 14:6)?

Dear Lord, you are, indeed, something else!

Amen.

LORD,

Pull me closer to you when I bake bread, cook spaghetti, make muffins, serve coffee, wash dishes, struggle with my computer, walk in the park, breathe fresh air, give away carrot juice, a pencil, a happy smile; when I share warmth, laughter, pain, a chicken dinner; when I add a little something in kindness to the lives of others—for that is "praying without ceasing" in action.

And help me to do all these little things the best I can, with great care and joy and attention, because who knows, *you* might be the one I am doing these little things for. Didn't you say, "Truly I tell you, just as you did it to one of the least of these who are members of my family, you did it to me" (Matthew 25:40)? So you are supposed to be the One I am doing these little things for. Am I right?

Lord, even though I can lose you every day in every thing, help me to find you every day and in every thing. For every day is your day, and every thing is your thing.

Please, Lord, help me to know you and love you in the ordinary, and to do the little things the way you would have done them yourself.

Please, Lord, make me live my life in ways that will let others recognize you in me.

Amen.

✦

LORD,

We know just a little about your angels—compared to what we know about your saints and other religious matters. Your angels chant your glory and serve you as messengers. Only three angels are mentioned by name in the Bible, and then only briefly. Gabriel interpreted the vision of Daniel and announced the birth of John the Baptizer and Jesus (see Daniel 8:16, 9:21; Luke 1:11-20, 1:26-38); Raphael protected Tobiah (see Tobit 12:15); and Michael protected the people of Israel (see Daniel 10: 13, 21). We also know that Joseph was going to take leave from Mary when the angel appeared to him and told him to change his mind. We know, too, that the angel instructed Joseph on protecting the child Jesus.

But, dear Lord, all the people who come into our lives when we are confused or in need—people who help us in any way to find our way, especially your way—aren't they angels, too?

Your angels must be everywhere, for you are everywhere. Your angels are those with whom we share our homes; they are our friends; they are those who will become our friends. Everyone carries a message for us and for others. They are there when we are sick, confused, happy, or experiencing deep joy. They are there at any time and in any place—but we often do not see them and do not listen to them.

Joseph listened to the angel. I need to listen to my angel, too.

Dear Lord, I am going to listen to my angel, just as Joseph listened to his. I am going to listen to what my angel says about your plans for my life, just as Mary listened to her angel about your plans for her life.

Amen.

LORD,

I want to tell you something. All those books that are about you do not mean much to me. In fact, most of the time I do not understand them and, often, they bore me.

You might be somewhere in these books, Lord, but I am sure you must be more present somewhere else. I know this, Lord.

I feel you with me when I go shopping, when I eat, drink, drive my old car, walk in the woods, go to work, witness a sunrise or sunset, play with sand on the shore, talk to my neighbor, laugh with old friends, or enjoy the top of the mountains, the depths of the valleys, the bird in flight, and the blooming red rose. Everywhere and at all times, dear Lord, I feel you with me.

Thank you, Lord, for having led my eyes to discern you in the immense simplicity of these little things.

I am sure you are there. I am sure you are not only in the books. I am sure you are everywhere. Make me a "walking theology" of life.

Amen.

✜

LORD,

I will do my part: I will sow a seed.

To sow a seed is to say "yes" to life.

A seed does not come from nothing, and it has the tree within—all the past and all the future. Debt and hope are in a seed.

I will sow a seed.

I will cooperate with your creation—with nature's work, your work—and declare the interdependence of all things. We all stand together or we all fall together.

I will sow a seed.

A seed is green earth, green consciousness, a new quality of life, a new beauty to the eye, uplifting to the spirit.

To sow a seed is to allow it to die in order to resurrect an infinite number of seeds.

I will give all my care to the seed. I will nurture the seed. But growth remains your gift, Lord, and the fruition of the seed needs your sun and your rain.

I will sow a seed. I will do my part. The rest is yours.

You are the very destiny of the seed. You are its growth, its generosity, its love.

I will sow a seed.

Amen.

✛

LORD,

There are so many choices in everyday living. There are so many decisions to make.

There are so many things going on in my life, so many pressures falling upon me from family, friends, school, work—and life itself.

There are within me so many needs: physical, emotional, intellectual, spiritual; so many ambitions and worries, too.

There is life—and then there is my little life.

And then there is *you.*

But why do they keep telling me that I have to choose you or choose life, when *you are life?*

Are you really different from my worries, my needs, my pressures, my ambitions? Are you really different from my life?

Am I holier when I am pure spirit? But I am a human being as once you were.

Am I closer to you when I disincarnate myself?

Lord, give me the wisdom to understand and do what you want in my life. Give me the wisdom to make the fundamental choice: to recognize you in every decision I have to make each day, for my seemingly futile decisions cease to be futile when you are within them.

Be *the decision* that gives meaning to all my other decisions, for you are my beloved Lord.

Amen.

✛

LORD,

I am thirsty, thirsty, thirsty and dying for you. Why don't you come?

I am restless, so restless that I don't really care much about food, sleep, power, money, fame—or about this and that. My whole concern is you.

On the surface, I see myself as utterly calm and quiet, but my heart is burning—on fire with love for you.

Without you, beloved Lord, only those who know what love is can understand what fire is, what pain is, and what suffering is.

Those who don't know the language of the heart are astonished to see me so silent, so still, for what they don't see—how can they see?—is that deep within I am carrying a storm.

Day in and day out, I think only of you.

I find myself rushing to see if you are there, coming with the wind that knocks on the door. And I wait. I've waited too long.

And with the wind, dry leaves move along the road. Again I rush, thinking that the sound of the moving leaves are the sounds of your footsteps.

And with the snow, I rush to the window to see if you are coming with the falling flakes.

And with the blooming flowers, I rush to see if you are coming in the fragrance of the blossoms.

And always there is something missing. The bride wants her lover—and the lover does not show up.

When you don't answer me while I go on calling you, Lord, doubts arise in me: Do my words reach you? Do you care about me? Is there somebody who will take the message to you? Otherwise, why don't you come?

I am thirsty for you, Beloved. I am thirsty for you. But I know—I know—my thirst is still not enough and my longing is not sufficiently intense, otherwise surely you would have come.

Dear Lord, my beloved Lord, make my thirst so intense that I become the host who is worthy of receiving you.

I am sure that you will come when I unlock my doors, when I wear my wedding garment, when the intensity of my longing becomes unbearable.

The sun does not enter the house if nobody invites it by opening the door.

Wouldn't you help me to open the door?

Amen.

LORD,

When I think about how we live our spiritual lives, I feel that we, in spite of all appearances, still are in the third world of spirituality.

When we say something like "the Son of Man is God" or when we talk about the Trinity, Revelation, Tradition, the grace of God, and all other dogmatic points we are supposed to believe in, we declare our affiliation to the Church we belong to. This is easy. Problems arise when our beliefs remain abstract, when they satisfy only the persons who formulated them. Faith becomes something ideal, an artificial means with no roots on earth. It ends up being detached, remote, unreal.

Lord, why am I "tortured" every day by people who want to know whether or not I believe in you? Why do they want to know my most intimate secrets? Why do they hurry to assure me of my salvation if my answer pleases them—and to guarantee my damnation if my answer repulses them? Isn't your gospel made to be breathed, eaten, drunk, merged with, replayed, reinvented, adjusted to, totally lived here and now?

Our mental certainties may satisfy our intelligence and bring money to our pockets, but they have no value if our perceptions and deeds do not confirm them.

If my faith does not speak out and act against prejudice and all kinds of injustices and barriers, and if it does not affect my relations with my neighbors and my "enemies," my faith is mere words.

Dear Lord, help me to lose this kind of "faith." What good is this kind of faith when it is a mere mental object, a system, a culture, an ideology, a source of income, a past, a tradition, a certain concept of the future, an escape?

I deserve better than this, Lord. You deserve better from me.

Let my faith be real, disturbing, electrifying. Let my faith be fire, within and without.

Dear Lord, I believe in you totally, completely, globally, unconditionally, whether or not I am intellectually satisfied. I believe in you with all my soul, heart, body, and actions. Henceforth, I want you to be in my personal history, as you are in human history. History, indeed, is not a simple collection of different events and conquests. Rather, history is the story of you with humankind. It is my story of trust in you.

Lord, when my turn comes, do not permit me to leave behind the same earth that was here when I came to it—for that would mean that I did not believe enough in you to help change it.

Lord, help me make of my faith a living-flesh faith. I want my faith to be my way of life, my personal history, and my contribution to human-divine history.

Amen.

✥

L<small>ORD</small>,

You said: "Whatever you ask for in prayer with faith, you will receive" (Matthew 21:22).

You also said: "For truly I tell you, if you have faith the size of a mustard seed, you will say to this mountain, 'Move from here to there,' and it will move; and nothing will be impossible for you" (Matthew 17:20).

And you also said: "Come to me, all you that are weary and are carrying heavy burdens, and I will give you rest" (Matthew 11:28).

Well, I am going to take you at your word: I come to you. At the present time, Lord, I am experiencing big problems with my family, my job, my relationships with others—and sometimes with myself and my health. I do not know what went wrong. This situation causes me a lot of headaches, anxieties, and worries, and I cannot handle all of them anymore. I turn them all over to you, without exception, and I turn myself over to you, too, totally and without restrictions.

I say this not only with conviction, but with all my being. I have total faith that you will do something. I believe you must do something. I believe you will do something.

I pray in depth, with all my being, like Peter when he was drowning: "Lord, save us! We are perishing!" (Matthew 8:25)

I am sure that the "sea" and the "winds" will "obey" you (see Matthew 8:27).

Amen.

LORD,

In reading Job's story, I wondered about who you really were.

I first thought—and I still do—that Job was a good servant of yours. He was a righteous person. "There is no one like him on the earth, a blameless and upright man who fears God and turns away from evil" (Job 1:8).

So why in the world did all kinds of catastrophes fall upon such a good man? Why?

His philosopher and theologian friends thought that you were all good and all powerful, therefore Job must not be too good—so he must repent.

These friends are not that foolish after all; they are reasonable. But they miss the point about Job.

Appearance is not reality; the obvious is not necessarily the solution. Life is not all problems to be solved; rather, life is a mystery to be lived.

Lord,

You are "absurd." Sometimes what you do does not seem rational, reasonable, predictable, comfortable, and convenient. The connection with you does not look like a formula or a prescription. But then, since when is a love story rational, with a clear map and without any risks?

I am, of course, grateful for all that you have given me. And I have been told that honesty, decency, intelligence, loyalty, goodness, and genuineness are somewhat exceptional in me. So why do things so often—most of the time, in fact—not go my way? Most of the time, the thief, the liar, the unjust, the opportunist, the violent, are the prosperous ones, the success-ful ones, the lucky ones, the powerful ones.

Frankly, I am shocked by your injustice, unfairness, and absurdity. I am shocked by you.

Like Job, I am experiencing your absence.

Where are you, dear Lord? Where are you?

And like Job, my love for you must be somehow infected with disappointment and perhaps even resentment. Do you blame me?

Are you testing me, Lord? For how long? Didn't I prove that I was faithful to you, as much as a human being can be faithful? My faith has not been because things are going well and it is in my own best interest to be faithful. Rather, my faith has been in the depth of my soul, even when faith seemed "absurd," when appearances contradicted reality, when things were really bad.

This sheer faith, when reason no longer has a say, must make sense. Right?

Like Job, I gave up the idea of pushing the right but-tons to obtain the right answers. You are neither in a library book nor on a computer disk. And you are not a machine. You defined yourself as "I am." Therefore you must be a "person," not just an "object." You cannot be a concept. All the mystics and saints who have met you could not find the right words to describe you.

It seems to me that "I" and "you" would become so con-nected that I would take them for one, no matter what. Then I would have not much to say, except that I must repent. Repent not because of a sin I have committed—although it could be—but because, deep down, I played God. I must shut up.

My words are empty speeches.

My words falsify the Word that you are.

Only silence allows your Word to speak.

Lao Tzu put it so well when he said: "Those who say don't know; those who know don't say."

Only when I shut up will you show up.

Lord,

And maybe, after all, it is not that important to have my questions answered. You chose to answer the questioner, not the questions. This is certainly a far better method. It took your infinite Love on the cross to convince me of this simple truth of your method.

Job said:

> "*I have uttered what I did not understand,*
> > *things too wonderful for me, which I did not know.*
> '*Hear, and I will speak;*
> > *I will question you, and you declare to me.*'
> *I had heard of you by the hearing of the ear,*
> > *but now my eye sees you*" (Job 42:3–5).

This was Job's final answer—and it is mine as well. Job did not understand; rather, he saw you. I do not understand; rather, I see you.

Then all my suspicions, dissatisfactions, disappointments, protests, and that feeling of being cheated and betrayed are dropped.

I see you, even in your "absence."

I see how bittersweet you are! Love is never boring.

Thank you, dear Lord, for being so involved.

Amen.

LORD,

I earnestly know that in the depth of my heart my culture does not fulfill my being. Even though I seem to like it at times, it does not satisfy my soul.

I like comfort. My culture values comfort over fulfillment.

I like the good life. My culture identifies the good life with earning big money, owning the large house and the new car, holding the high position, and enjoying the luxury vacation.

I like to be happy. My culture, even though it pushes me to dream about overnight successes, fast food, fifteen-second cold relief, and instant anything, does not deliver exactly what it promises; the gratification always remains around the corner or over the next hill. And I do have that tendency to say:

"I'll be happy when I make a million a year."

"I'll be happy when I have a second (summer/winter) home."

"I'll be happy when I get that promotion."

"I'll be happy when I get married/separated."

"I'll be happy when the kids are out of school."

And somehow, that happiness is always in the future— never now. It's always in some achievement that can never live up to the expectation imagined.

I also like the luxuries of modern life. My culture lets me take for granted things like automobiles, televisions, radios, dishes, washing machines, telephones, stereos, central heat, air conditioning, movies, theaters, restaurants, travel. But what is the point of all this?

I've been using all these things for a long time and yet, this has been only a part of my "American dream." What is the point, if they do not give me the happiness I am looking for?

They taught me a lesson, however, an old lesson that I'll never forget: "Joy is not in things; it is in us." The "American dream" of happiness must not be in the "next thing" or in the "ever after" or in this or that possession.

Dear Lord,

Allow me to identify exactly my "American dream": reaching the Infinite, you, and living it totally, globally, and continuously. Is there another way of being really happy? Lord, you are the way.

Amen.

LORD,

This morning I felt like I had nothing to say—so I didn't talk to you as I usually do. In fact, I didn't talk to anyone.

On my way home from work, however, I saw a vendor of beautiful flowers. I stopped, bought a bunch of those beautiful flowers, took it to our church—which is not far from my house—and put it on the altar.

Amen.

LORD,

For a long time I prayed for security. I devoutly asked for personal security, economic security, national security, environmental security, intellectual security, emotional security—even spiritual security. I wanted to insure my place on earth as well as in heaven. I thought that, like James and John (see Matthew 20:21), this was the right thing to do.

But then I read your gospel again, dear Lord, and realized that security was not part of your life. "The foxes have lairs, the birds in the sky have nests, but the Son of Man has nowhere to lay his head" (Matthew 8:20). Then, later on, in the Garden of Gethsemani, your closest friends went to sleep and you had to face your suffering alone. Then you were betrayed by one of your own disciples and denied by another, and you vulnerably submitted yourself to the killing wounds.

Lord, security was not what you were looking for. Rather, you dared to believe totally in God's providential love. You were vulnerable to God, the Father.

As your follower, I feel challenged by your gospel and your way of life. I always thought that security is what I needed most, to be able to do what you call me to do. But I am challenged to believe that God is walking with me into the dry desert of temptations, the lonely gardens of Gethsemani, and the cruel Golgotha of the crucifixion in my own life. And like you and Abraham before you, I sometimes feel called to pick up and go, I do not really know where, trusting that God is there leading me somewhere to a new job, a new country, a new lifestyle, a new way of thinking. I just have to trust God;

I have to be vulnerable to his providence. Then I can be vulnerable before myself, by dropping my many masks and lies and pretensions, and by realizing my own limitations—the way I really am. Then I can be vulnerable before others by accepting them as "different." You, yourself, Lord, reached out to the lepers and the paralyzed, the diseased and the demonics, the outcasts and the foreigners, the Canaanites and the Samaritans, the tax collectors and the sinners. And by doing so, you risked the comfort of your personal security and the security of public approval. You dared! You were so vulnerable before the Father's will.

Lord, help me to understand that when I enter into a relationship with a broken human being, it is me who is healed first.

Lord, make me fully human—I mean vulnerable and affected by life, persons, and events. And make me strong enough to affect them, too. I am what I am only in relationship to all others, events, and circumstances in the world around me. I am what I am only when I am vulnerable to you and to others—for my relationship to you and to others is not something added to me. Rather, it is me. The risk of vulnerability and the ability to be wounded *is* my real security.

Please, Lord, let me understand that I cannot heal without accepting the possibility of being hurt, as you were hurt so many times.

Amen.

LORD,

From the days of my childhood, I have felt a thirst, a longing for something. I have never known what this thirst is and, although I have pursued it almost my entire life, I've never succeeded in reaching it. How can I catch what I don't know what I am seeking?

The one thing I know, however, is that this mysterious impulse draws my heart and my soul entirely and passionately. It drives my entire being to search, and I feel as though I will have no rest before I've achieved it.

Lord,

I've tried, since the beginning, to satisfy this thirst by seeking created things. I also tried different lifestyles, countries, and universities, thinking I would find the answer that would quench my thirst someplace there. But the more I sought, the less I was able to find—and the nearer I thought I was, the further I was from it. It seems the more I know, the less I am sure. And the more I accumulate things, the less secure in life I become.

Now, Lord, my whole being is in turmoil. I cannot live with it; I cannot live without it.

Lord,

What is this?
What is this thirst, this longing, made of?
What is going on in me?
What is it that is hidden in me?

What is it that is playing tricks on me?

You are the one I have been looking for, for so long—aren't you?

My soul thirsts for you.

Answer me, Lord. Please answer me.

Amen.

LORD,

This morning, when I tried to stand up automatically by myself, alone, I felt a pain on my knee.

I was in a hurry. I did not think of you. I counted on myself alone—and when we count on ourselves, forgetting that you are there, we are going to be hurt sooner or later. But let me tell you this. Thank you for the gift of pain. Pain means there is something that needs to be fixed. Pain means that we need to pay attention to what we are doing. Pain especially indicates your deep love for us.

I am sure that this morning you were helping me avoid a greater pain that could have been catastrophic. Pain reminds me that you want to be involved with me in all that I am doing.

Okay, Lord!

Now let's fix this problem. They tell me that I need an operation and must stay home from work for several weeks. If you want to be involved, be involved. Here is a good opportunity. I badly need your help.

Naturally, I hope you will decide that an operation is not necessary. But if an operation is, in fact, necessary, help me to believe that the hands of that doctor who is going to operate on me are your loving hands.

When love is there, hurt is no longer hurt.

Please, Lord, send an angel to take care of my knee.

Please, Lord, be totally involved with my own things, big and small, now and always.

Amen.

LORD,

That pain in my knee does not go away. It's been with me seven weeks. Isn't that enough, dear Lord?

I concede that it is not an unbearable pain. Still, I cannot walk the stairs as I normally do. I cannot walk outdoors more than one or two hours at a time—and this means that I cannot go to work and perform the way I am expected to perform, the way I am used to performing. It is humbling.

But let me be positive, dear Lord, and say that pain, in a sense, is a sign of aliveness. Right? When we are no longer alive, we no longer feel pain. The more sensitive to pain we are, the more vulnerable we become—and the more alive. Isn't this the very reason we sometimes are afraid of being truly alive?

Being truly alive means being more sensitive, more vulnerable and, therefore, more subject to pain. This is why we are afraid of changing our habits and routines. We are afraid of loving. We are afraid of being transformed. We are afraid of letting you be too involved in our lives. For who knows what will happen then?

Lord, let my pain make me more alive. Let everything in my life contribute to my being fully alive. Your friend, Irenaeus, said it so well long ago: "The glory of God is a human being who is fully alive." Then I will be real—and when we are truly and fully alive and real, we feel things even more painfully. But then, being truly and fully alive, we do not mind feeling pain.

Pain hurts. Pain hurts much less, however, if it begets aliveness, if it makes us more authentic, more real.

Pain—any pain—can open our eyes to something we didn't see before. Pain can help us determine what is essential in our lives. When this happens, we may even forget the process. The blind person in John's Gospel said: "One thing I do know, that though I was blind, now I see" (9:25).

Lord,

Let me be closer to you after this pain.

Let me be more alive, more sensitive, and more loving to others in pain.

Let me be more real.

Let me see what you want me to see.

Amen.

LORD,

Tomorrow I am going to the hospital—surgery is necessary—and I feel terribly lonely. My parents are no longer with us, and all my relatives are far away. I have some friends, though, but they are there especially for good times; their number decreases in bad times.

I am not afraid, though, Lord. I have one great friend who will never leave me alone, even if sometimes I ask him to leave me alone. He is always there—and he will be there with me tomorrow. He will come with his angels to watch over me and the doctor and the nurses. He will be there. He often goes to hospitals, so I am sure he will be there—perhaps even before I get there.

Although he is a tricky person, I love him very much. He helps me a lot. I said tricky—he really is. He allowed me to have a pain on my right knee for some reason that I don't know yet.

Maybe he wanted to prevent me having a much greater problem. Maybe he wanted me to feel how important each part of my body is. After all, we take everything for granted.

From now on I am going to say, "Thank you, Lord, for every cell of my body, from the top of my head to the bottom of my heel. Thank you for keeping me healthy on this earth. You are my wonderful friend, Lord."

Amen.

That Knee

LORD,

My knee hurts so much that I can't sleep at night. Is this what you want, dear Lord?

I felt nothing the day of the operation. The doctor, the nurses, and the angels you sent moved my leg whichever way they wanted. As I watched them on the monitor, I thought they were working on someone else's knee. They could have done anything; they could have cut off my leg altogether. For about three hours, it seemed that my leg did not belong to me.

That day, dear Lord, I felt an extreme necessity for my leg; it became the most important member of my entire body. Now I know that I need my leg to get up in the morning, to go to the bathroom, to go downstairs, to go to the kitchen, to drive my car, to go to work, to go shopping, to have a nice walk, to play tennis, to swim, to enjoy life. I used to take all this for granted. How silly I was!

It took an operation to be able to feel the great importance of my knee.

I need my hand to be able to write what I am writing.

I need my eyes to be able to see what and why I am writing.

I need my ears, my nose, my skin, my hair—all of myself.

How many times a day, Lord, do we hear about the "perfect body"? How come we still forget the wonder of how the muscles work, how the knees and fingers flex, how the hair grows, how the stomach digests foods, how we breathe, how we see, taste, sense things, how we are able to walk, run, sit, and stand? This truly is an incredible work of art—a miracle! The entire body is a miracle!

Lord, help me to realize the beauty and immense complexity of each and every cell of my body, mind, heart, and soul. Help me to heal the division between spirit and matter, by bringing them together into unifying prayer. Make my body a sacred temple.

Yes, I want to pray to you with my entire being, dear Lord. Yes, I want to accept your invitation to participate with you in the exciting, beautiful, challenging, and often painful journey of life. Yes, I want to live the mystery of your Incarnation that is continuing here and now. You are where I am, in all situations. You, yourself, took our skin, spoke our language, ate our foods, breathed our air, walked our roads. Help me to find you clearly in this painful experience of my life, where I am right now.

I am aware now of the importance of every detail in my life.

How wonderful you are, dear Lord! Thank you for all your gifts, one by one. Help me to stay healthy, for health is a blessing that money cannot buy.

True health is having you live within me. Then I am a new creation in you.

Amen.

✛

GOD,

    Almighty Lord, Creator:

    All things are yours—

        the fresh morning,

        the relaxing evening,

        the day and night,

        the sun, the moon,

        light and darkness,

        the vibrant grass and the scent of flowers,

        the peaceful breeze and the solidity of the mountain,

        the changing seasons and the permanence of life,

        the shifting beauty of the hills and the profound

            purple valleys,

        the ocean, the waves, and the golden rays,

        the depth of the eyes in a human face,

        the spontaneity of a warm pet.

    All of them are yours.

        All beauty is yours.

        The heavens declare your glory and the earth

            witnesses your love.

    And I live in this magic garden of your creation.

But, Lord,

    Creation does not look perfect; it is always threatened
by the shadow of decay.

        In the green leaves, there is the prospect of falling

            yellow ones.

In the serenity of that face, there are always the
   wrinkles of the passing time.
In the flower, there is always some kind of thorn.
There are always thorns in that garden we live in.
Always there are some kinds of thorns.

Lord, the Almighty,
   You are the nucleus of life,
      the core of being,
      the energy of renewal,
      and the essence of the perennial.
   You are the beauty of beauty,
      the caring thorn,
      and the falling leaf that points the way home.
   You are the one beyond any apparent duality and
beyond obvious opposites.
   You are the paradox, the ecstasy of the paradox, the
only real ecstasy.
   Thank you, Lord, for giving me the chance to see you
everywhere and to have a foretaste of you here and now.
   Amen.

✣

All Things Are Yours

LORD,

When I go to church on Sunday morning, I instantly ask you to forgive me, for I am a sinner. This is what I am supposed to do, I guess. It is in the prayer ritual, the liturgical request.

But do I really mean it?

Perhaps not, because I really do not perceive myself as a sinner. I do not stop and look into the depths of my soul. I may go to church believing that I am worshiping God when, in fact, my mind and heart are elsewhere—much concerned with my television set I just bought, my red car, my beautiful house, my rewarding job, my respected routine to come to church, my own notions of God and of truths.

Yet, aren't all these things, after all, golden calves? Prejudice is an important part of my life, and I didn't know it. I do not mean I discriminate. No, I deeply respect all races, nationalities, genders, minorities, and differences. I've never had problems with these differences. But I've never stopped and looked at a more subtle prejudice: the spiritual prejudice.

When I am convinced that I am right and everybody else is wrong, when I am certain that my way of worshiping and doing things is the only way, when my concept of God prevails over others' concepts of God, and when I do what I do on my own, without bothering to mention your name and ask for help, I repeat what the Israelites did in the Old Testament, when Moses left them and went to the mountain. They started to worship golden calves—and this is what I do, too.

Lord, open my eyes and help me see things as they really are. Show me your true face, others' true faces, and my true face.

Lord, if I sleep, please do not sleep. Someone has to watch over me.

Please, Lord, watch over me. Be in my head, my thoughts, my heart, my feelings, my mouth, my words, my hands, my feet, my acts. Be in everything—everything.

I pray to you, dear Lord, with all my virtues and especially with all my sins, known and unknown.

Forgive me, Lord, for I am a sinner. I really see my sins today and I really ask your forgiveness for the ones written in the ritual and the ones that are very personal.

Amen.

✛

LORD,

Our world is becoming more and more complex and sophisticated. It is supposedly more secure for human beings.

But when we think about this, we can become dizzy and somehow feel ironically insecure. Changes and shifting values and lifestyles scare us, don't they.

Probably, this is why we reassure ourselves by buying all kinds of insurance. This is why, more than ever before, we seek out gurus, spiritual leaders, ideologies, systems, schools of thoughts—anything that looks solid.

Even the computers and the latest technology do not bring answers about our security. Our jobs, on which we are counting, can be lost overnight as a result of decisions over which we have no control.

The eternal questions remain the same. In fact, they seem more eternal than ever. What's to become of me? What is life all about? Where did I come from? Why am I here now? Where am I going? How will I get there? Who am I?

I'm crying out to you, Lord. All my insurances and explanations are futile. You are my only security. You are my compass, my friend, my guide on this journey. You are the answer.

Lord, let me live, in the most concrete way, what I just affirmed.

Amen.

✛

L ORD,

I am thirsty—thirsty for your infinite love. Why don't you come to me?

I warmly invite you to visit me.

Come, dear Lord, to my heart. Be my living water.

My door is open for you. My mind, my heart, my soul are open for you. I am ready for you.

Come.

I am thirsty for you. Please, Lord, come.

My thirst, and nothing else, is my only qualification for your coming.

I remember what you said:

> *"I am the Alpha and the Omega, the Beginning and the End. To anyone who thirsts I will give to drink without cost from the spring of lifegiving water"* (see Revelation 21:6).

I do not deserve that you visit me, dear Lord. I cannot afford your precious visit. But, come. My burning thirst for you is my only qualification for your visit.

Please, Lord, bring with you this "without cost" drink you were talking about. Nothing in the world can replace it— not one single thing. Not even all things put together.

Your infinite love comes "without cost."

Your infinite love comes only when we are truly thirsty.

Now I see what Augustine meant when he said: *"Ama et fac quod vis"* ("Love and do what you will").

My dear beloved Lord,

Make my love for you all-inclusive, global, and total. Make my entire being capable of much more passion, intimacy, and joy through you, in you, by you, and for you. My thirst is so deep and inextinguishable that only you can satisfy it.

Make me say, as loudly as I can and with great meaning, as truly as I am able: "My beloved is mine and I am his" (Song of Solomon 2:16).

My thirst is so great that only you—you—can extinguish it.

My thirst—my deepest yearning—is my only qualification for you, my beloved Lord.

Amen.

LORD,

Very often I find it difficult to follow you. Sometimes I do not even understand what you are talking about, and I frequently look for you in the wrong places.

However, do not think that I am lazy. I always did—and still do—my homework well. I worked hard at it.

For many years I read book after book after book.

I frequented retreat centers and guest houses.

I asked priests, ministers, spiritual directors, sages, mystics, and those who withdraw in a complete monastic life, mortifying the flesh and dedicating their entire lives to prayer and silence.

I was ready, like most seekers, to do everything and anything, even at great cost to myself and my checkbook, to find the right path to you. I asked them all to draw me the map that leads to you—a way to you without errors and delays.

They explained to me how to reach my destination. They indicated privileged situations in which human beings encountered you. They talked with eloquence about prayer, the interior life, asceticism, the simple lifestyle, unselfishness, the Church and its sacraments, and the love of neighbor. And all of them insisted on following the gospel.

I tried to do just that, and I am still trying.

But at a certain point, when I was going back and forth to meet with these people, I wondered why I did not stop to help that street person or the bag lady on my way to the retreat center. Perhaps I was afraid to be late—or maybe there was some other reason. Perhaps I took another route altogether, avoiding that part of the city where society's ills are so manifest. I also recalled how, with much anger and resentment, I criticized my landlords for not providing me the respect I thought I was entitled.

Lord,

I have thought about the map that all your qualified people—your professionals—have shown me. I appreciate what they have said to me. But I wonder if you might have another map, one a little less sophisticated.

Aren't you in the kindness I should have had with my landlords?

Aren't you in the warmth of a sincere smile and a welcoming word to a stranger?

Aren't you in a good belly laugh, when a trusted friend relieves my worries?

Aren't you in the concern of an employer for an employee, and in the dedication of an employee for an employer?

Aren't you in the loving heart of a nurse who listens to an anxious patient?

Aren't you present in every human activity, be it in offices, schools and universities, hospitals, stores, hotels, factories, restaurants, farms, cities, suburbs, streets—everywhere?

Aren't you where political decisions are made: in the state legislatures, in offices of responsibility, in courts, in conference rooms, and in executive suites?

Aren't you there when a realtor makes an honest sale?

The Map That Leads to You

Aren't you there when an ambulance team responds efficiently to a critical situation?

Aren't you there when a good neighbor goes on an errand for an elderly person?

Aren't you there when someone takes care of the lonely, the helpless, the ill, the homeless, the brokenhearted, the hungry?

Aren't you in what I think and how I think, in what I say and how I say it, in what I do and how I do it?

Isn't it a lie to separate worship from regular daily life and work? Are you really more present in the sanctuary than in the street? What is the meaning of a sacrament if I do not learn to live it in my daily life? Can I really share the eucharistic meal with others without being willing to share other meals as well? What is the meaning of our liturgy if I detach it from life and the world?

Lord,

I certainly have the right reverence to the church space. I bow in reverence before your cross and have great respect for the images and statues of your saints. I kiss my bishop's ring. But shouldn't I have the same reverence for each person in whom you dwell, by not tolerating hunger, oppression, injustice, ignorance, slavery, racism, and hatred? Should the images made of wood and the statues made of marble receive greater respect than human beings who are your living images? Shouldn't our planet be treated with the respect we have for church buildings? Shouldn't we heal the polluted land, water, and air?

Lord,

When you created the world, you declared it good. How come we've had the audacity and shamelessness to correct you by distorting your geography and deciding where the holy is and is not to be found?

Dear Lord,

Forgive me for having put you behind the sacristy door for too long. It was safer for you, and it was safer for me, too. Now I know. How could I have ignored it? Nothing ought to be just secular and no place is excluded from being a holy place.

Lord,

The map to you, contrary to what I first thought, is open and accessible to anyone. Holiness must not be associated with only those who pursue it as a clerical profession. It is not the monopoly of monks and cloistered nuns who chant the Divine Office in the wee hours of the morning. Holiness is the call and obligation of all people, wherever they happen to be and whatever God wants them to be doing for his glory. The true touchstone for holiness is how we treat one another and the world. This is your teaching, Lord: "I desire mercy, not sacrifice" (Matthew 9:13, see also 12:7). And I am going to stick with what you've said to us.

Now I feel, more than ever before, that I am on the right path toward you. What I began with, as a pursuit of holiness, must have been a certain self-satisfaction and gratification from performing some kind of spiritual achievement. Holiness is certainly my union with you, with all my heart and soul and mind. But, "Those who do not love a brother or sister whom they have seen, cannot love God whom they have not seen" (1 John 4:20). So now it is becoming crystal clear: The map to you is my neighbor's face and place. Period.

Please Lord,
> Make me holy through loving my neighbor.
> Amen.

LORD,

Today was a wonderful day! Everything seemed in good order. Everything was as it should be. No complaints. Nothing.

Thank You!

But how can I make it last? Can I recreate it tomorrow? And is this all there is? In spite of all my satisfactions, a profound hunger haunts my heart and soul. I also see this same hunger everywhere around me.

Why is everyone looking for "something more"?

Why is everyone trying to find ways to feel unique and important in who they are and in what they do?

Why is everyone running after more money, more experiences, more knowledge, more power, more connections—more anything?

Even when life seems to be going along wonderfully, why do people still feel dissatisfied and want more, more, and more?

In today's world, high-tech conditions are continually changing, values are questioned, uncertainties are prevailing, relationships are becoming more fragile than ever, and chaos rather than a new world order seems to be taking place everywhere, in every culture.

What is the meaning of all our satisfactions and all our dissatisfactions?

What is the point of it all?

Lord,

When you, the Son of God, chose to take the form of our bodies some two thousand years ago, Mary and Joseph were not able to find a single room in the local inn in Bethlehem. So you had to be born in a cave and laid in a manger. Just as Bethlehem was overcrowded two thousand years ago, the hearts of men and women are still overcrowded by concerns other than you: "Can't you see how busy I am, Lord?" "My schedule is full for two months, Lord." "I am going on a business trip, Lord." "I have more important things to do, Lord." "I am building a new house, Lord." "I am writing a new book, Lord." "I am busy making money, Lord." So "I have no room for you, Lord."

Worldly concerns can provide only partial and temporary satisfactions to a heart hungry for the Infinite.

Also, your birth was not first announced to the great ones of this world—those who have the answers for everything. No, your birth would not have been understood by the people who know everything. Only shepherds and wise men can understand your birth. Shepherds know that they know nothing, and wise men know that they do not know much. Shepherds and wise men are humble. They do not pretend. They wonder. They understand the mystery that is hidden to those who think that they are above the rest of us, those who have the answer for everything.

Lord,

"What is the point of it all?"

"Is this all there is?"

This year, let your Christmas be a beginning of a continuous Christmas in my life.

Let me realize, like the shepherds and the wise men, that I do not have all the answers. And, unlike overcrowded Bethlehem, let me make room for you in my heart, so that your light will help me to sort my "overcrowded" concerns and cares of this world and understand the point of it all.

Amen.

LORD,

Frankly, I sometimes do not feel your presence around here. I pray and pray and pray—and nothing seems to move or be removed. Even the comfort of being under your guidance seems to evaporate. I've already told you hundreds of times about my problems, and you seem so far away, so aloof, so indifferent. Nothing changes. There was great success before—so why have things gone wrong all of a sudden?

Now I am tired. I am irritable. I am losing energy. I used to enjoy life, to be on top of everything—but now I seem to drive myself burdensomely to do that which used to be enjoyable. For example, I used to enjoy writing letters, especially to some of my family members and friends. Now I hardly write a good and happy letter to any of them. I seem to have been harboring dark shadows of bitterness and resentment—even though I don't want to admit it—because some of the people closest to me were elsewhere when I needed them most. My longtime cherished and treasured closeness to them took a sudden turn, and was perhaps even shattered. Something went wrong. What a loss! What a shame! I feel very sad, disappointed, and angry. Why should this happened to me? Why should I feel like I'm in a barren, dry, lonely, desert? Why?

Now I come to you, Lord, even though I never left you. Where to go? I have nowhere else to go.

"Remove this cup from me" (Mark 14:36). In other words, "Get me out of this impasse!" This is my raw cry for help. This is my visceral longing for transformation. "Get me out of this!"

I am sure that "for you all things are possible" (Mark 14:36). So why don't you want to take me out of this impasse? Why? And even if I say, "Yet, not what I want, but what you want" (Mark 14:36), I still hope and strongly wish this cup of impasse will be taken away.

And I will wait and pray.

No! I am not going to be like Judas, whose biggest sin was not betraying his Master but failing to hold on until the forgiveness and the glory of Sunday. The joy of Easter Sunday overcame by far the agony and the death of Friday. Judas, however, chose the despair of the impasse. I'll choose the hope of Sunday. No, I am not going to do what Judas did.

Lord, I am coming to you as Mary Magdalene did, "while it was still dark" (John 20:1), "weeping" (John 20:11). Her tears, as are mine, were tears of not only mourning but also confusion, consternation, embarrassment, loss of meaning, amazement, and disbelief. The very source of hope wasn't there. "They have taken the Lord out of the tomb!" (John 20:2).

Lord, I am more and more sure that we are so limited in space, time, conditions, and situations in life. We think that death is final, that our own case might be hopeless, and that we are on our own. We really are, but only if we depend on our own resources, systems, interests, and definitions. Judas did this—but Mary waited. Mary "saw" the Easter coming after the Good Friday.

The "dark" can be a source of illumination. Real healing is at the level of the dark unconsciousness more than at the level of a bright consciousness. Life instinct is deeper than logical understanding. Faith and love are stronger than definitions and superficial temporary satisfactions. The seed grows in the dark of the earth. The child develops in the dark womb. The scientist explores the dark unknown. The mystic finds illumination in the dark night of the soul. From the dark new things come to life. Hope is the fire of my faith, and trust is my way.

Lord,

Please, transform my Friday impasse into Easter Sunday glory.

Please forgive my disappointment of you.

Let me see the Easter spiritual growth that comes out of this Friday impasse.

Make of my desert an oasis, and of my impasse an opportunity for glorious transformation.

Let me feel your divine presence everywhere, even in your absence, when you seem so far away.

Let me understand that by surrendering to you, broken things can be mended, lost things can be found, questions can be answered, problems can be solved. You said: "I am the resurrection and the life. Those who believe in me, even though they die, will live, and everyone who lives and believes in me will never die" (John 11: 25–26).

Lord, I believe in you.

Amen.

LORD,

I often feel like I'm living life as if I were going on a one-way trip—there is no round-trip ticket. There is no way back to the "good old days," the way things used to be. I do not feel like I have a specific and clear destination—but I do know that "the way I was" is over.

I left home a long time ago.

Real faith involves leaving home.

Like Abraham, I left home in response to a fresh call from above. I left my temporary homeland, roles, jobs, relationships, ways of thinking, lifestyle, and belief systems. I left everything behind to go in search of my "promised land," the shining city, the kingdom of God.

I left behind my security and those life agendas that no longer fulfilled my deep desires. The temporary became the permanent, and the anywhere the somewhere.

This is a frightening situation. It is risky to live my faith. Not knowing what to expect next is scary.

But I remember what you said to your disciples: "If anyone comes to me without turning his back on his father and mother, his wife and his children, his brothers and sisters, indeed his very self, he cannot be my follower" (see Luke 14:26). To me, this means that I should let go of my old patterns of perceiving things and move to a new way of "seeing," perceiving, and living. And this is exactly what I am trying to do. My only light is my faith in you. Faith, somehow, makes every structure in my life provisional.

It wasn't easy to leave home. Leaving home is a death for yesterday, a loss for what was dear to me. It is painful to leave behind habits and all that one used to be. Oh, how many times I thought about what the Israelites said to Moses when they were too thirsty in the desert: "Why did you bring us out of Egypt, to kill us and our children and livestock with thirst?" (Exodus 17:3) But then I remembered what was said elsewhere: "Call to me and I will answer you, and will tell you great and hidden things that you have not known" (Jeremiah 33:3).

So I went on. I left. And I no longer regret having left.

The art of leaving is to create space for another to be, to develop, and to grow. I wanted you to grow within me. I wanted to be able to say what Paul wrote: "It is no longer I who live, but it is Christ who lives in me" (Galatians 2:20) or "Your attitude must be that of Christ" (see Philippians 2:5).

What was your attitude, dear Lord?

You, too, left the security of your heavens to become flesh, one of us (see John 1:14), with all the risks of vulnerability and human failure. There was not even room for you in the Bethlehem inn; you had to take a stable as a temporary shelter. You became a baby, totally dependent on others, and you never had a place to lay your head. You were always on the road, seeking to save the lost sheep and bringing the Good News to everyone. And the Good News was not only that we should love God, but that God loves us unconditionally and without ending and seeks to make of our living on earth a living similar to the one in heaven.

Lord, you showed us the way home.

Dear Lord,

Because I now know my destination, help me to go home to myself and find you in all the contours of my life. Indeed, you weave the threads of difficulties, challenges, joys, and blessings in my life. I know it.

Let me see what is invisible to my eyes.

Let me believe what is incredible to my mind.

Let me feel what is unbelievable to my heart.

Let me do what is impossible to my human power.

With you, indeed, nothing is impossible.

I want to give no more "thought to what lies behind but push on to what is ahead" (see Philippians 3:13).

I am a pilgrim in a faith journey.

I am in a continuous inner emigration.

I am your follower.

Help me to know exactly what your plans are for my life so that I might be what you want me to be.

Let me be able to say loudly, "The life I live now is not my own, Christ is living in me. I still live my human life but it is a life of faith in the Son of God, who loved me and gave himself for me" (see Galatians 2:20)—and let me be what I said I am. Let me realize, as concretely as possible, that the relationship I have with you is not something added to my humanness but is, actually, the very definition of it. For wholeness with you is the reality of my humanness. Therefore it is my personal and social reality.

Lord, be our reality.

Amen.   ✛

LORD,

The area where you wanted me to live is so beautiful. Besides its green hills, there is a breathtaking lake. How extraordinary is this combination of water and hills and trees—and colors and colors and colors! It is a postcard signed and delivered by you.

My lake is like a mirror. It is blue, green, red, yellow, and white, and it reflects that which is. It does not lie. It cannot lie. It reflects the majestic hills, the green trees, the imperious rocks, the blooming flowers, the deep sky, the playful clouds—just as they are. It tells the story of the golden sun all day long. It tells the story of the silver moon and the inviting stars, the silence of the peaceful night all night long. My lake enjoys the tender touch of the refreshing breeze and cherishes the subtle strikes of the gentle wind.

My lake is receptive. It allows anything in, and nothing alters its beauty. Should one throw a stone upon the lake, the stone will wound the face of the lake—but the lake, in a few seconds, forgives and loves again. The goodness and beauty of my lake are more rooted than a passing wound.

My lake is stronger than rock. Rock does not wear down its water; rather, water wears down rock. Rock breaks apart when hit by a hammer, but that hammer gets rusty if it hits my lake.

My lake extinguishes my thirst. It cleanses my body and relaxes my nerves and muscles. My lake rejuvenates my energy and makes me fresh again and again and again.

Lord,

As the lake, I want to be receptive to your graces and reflect your presence in my life and my behaviors. Let me be your mirror.

As the lake, I want to learn to be so flexible that I can face the overwhelming contradictions of life.

As the lake, I want to identify with not only the surface of my Christian life but also with the stillness below the surface, which is less turbulent. For there you are the Master of the house. You are the core of my being. Let me identify with the reservoir of awareness residing below the surface.

Lord,

Let me learn to sit in still awareness and convince myself that there is no other way in life to go except to the depths of my lake and my life, for this is where you are and where, in silence, you speak to me.

Wherever I happen to be, let me have in mind the image of my lake.

Let me stay fresh, with innocent eyes. Otherwise how can I reflect your divine presence and infinite beauty to others?

Thank you, Lord, for the lake that you have given me.

Amen.

LORD,

The mountain must have something special that other places seem not to have.

Since the beginning, mountains have been sacred places. Mount Olympus, for example, was the dwelling place of the gods.

The mountains are mentioned in the Bible so many times. Mount Sinai was the place where Moses received the commandments from God. You used to withdraw to the mountaintop by yourself to pray (see Matthew 14:23; Mark 6:46; Luke 6:12), to take a rest (see Matthew 15:29), to sit down with your disciples (see John 6:3) and have a talk with them (see Matthew 28:16), to transfigure (see Luke 9:29–36), to give the most important sermon in history (see Matthew 5–7). So many saints throughout history were attracted to the mountains and had their hermitages there.

The mountain is rock-solid. It has majesty and embodies calm and simplicity. On the mountain, one is in direct touch with unpolluted nature, fresh air, and pure water. On the mountains, one can rest and be inspired.

The mountain is a place of vision. Being on the mountain, or in sight of a mountain, is powerful—and even more powerful is the inner vision of the mountain and what it means to me.

The mountain is so massive, so solid, so unmoving.

The mountain has eternal white snow on its top and dancing green trees at its foot. It displays many peaks and has stillness, tranquility, and silence.

Lord,

As the mountain, I ask that you grant me the gift of stillness, centering, rootedness, and stable presence in the world.

As the mountain, I ask that you teach me to sit while the sun travels in the sky. In this same stillness, rooted in you, let me observe and enjoy the changing colors of life, the lights and shades of knowledge, and the moment-to-moment succession of emotions. Let me abide in you when the seasons flow into one another and the wind blows from all sides.

As the mountain, I ask that you let me be myself, in sunny days as well as in rainy days, in broiling temperatures as well as in frigid situations, when the roads are foggy and zigzagged and when they are clear and straight. Let me be myself when violent storms rage and when the birds of spring start to sing again; during the green season and when the yellow leaves start to fall. Through it all, allow me to continue to sit there, untouched by the world of changing appearances, for I am in touch with you, dear Lord, the Source of all things.

When my emotional storms and crises and thoughts and feelings are stronger than high winds, give me the strength and stability of the mountain. Help me to remain stable when my contradictions overwhelm me, and flexible when my unrealistic stubbornness leads me into dead-end roads.

When I deal with you and your eternal truths that I must live, make me like a rocky mountain: firm, uncompromising.

The Mountain Lesson

When I deal with my fellow human beings and their transient certainties—for they may not know what they are doing—make me a breezy mountain: soft, gentle, and flowing. Make me a solid mountain. Make me a breathing mountain. Make me a dancing mountain. Make me an intriguing mountain—ever changing and ever still.

Dear Lord,
Allow me to learn to be like a mountain.
Amen.

LORD,

When I was a child, one of my favorite things to do was to sit by a fireplace. The fireplace was such a comfort to me. It was a source of heat and light and inspiration, a place to dream and play. My uncle's stories around the fireplace were so intriguing and delightful. Imagination and dreams were more intense there. Reality wasn't real there—not at that time.

The fireplace also provided me with a certain courage. I used to hate the darkness because it scared me to death. After all, one doesn't know what is hidden in the darkness. The only way to fight darkness was the fire I used to have in my fireplace. Darkness would vanish at the first flame of the fire, and with it my fear.

Today, a fireplace in the house becomes just a luxury item, another piece of furniture. In this fastpaced world, few of us want to sit still; few of us like just to "be." Most of us try to fill all the available hours with busyness or noise. A simple touch of a switch, and we have the light we want and the heat we want and, eventually, all that which our materialistic world says we should want and need. We can, if we choose, become bombarded by sounds and images that come through electronic devices. So why bother with the stillness of a fireplace? Because we are becoming sophisticated people, stillness is a challenge.

Lord,

Even though I like this high-tech civilization, I want to ask you not to take away from me the warmth of a fireplace.

Put into me a passionate fire, for nothing can be done properly without the fire of passion. Love, for example, is not possible without the flame of passion. Maybe this is why you said: "I came to bring fire to the earth . . . Do you think that I have come to bring peace to the earth? No, I tell you, but rather division" (Luke 12:49, 51).

Dear Lord,

I thought you were the Prince of Peace, and here you are announcing fire and division. How in the world can you connect yourself with fire and division? Didn't you think it was nicer to savor the stillness and warmth of the fireplace?

Only when I think of the positive side of the fire does my confusion vanish. Fire has energy—a certain cleansing power. It gives warmth, light, and an invitation to a passionate life.

But it seems that you didn't come to make me comfortable but to bring me into new life. This means that I must get rid of my old stuff. How painful! Only fire can transmute my old stuff into a new way of life, as it transmutes metals.

You allowed division in me, between my deepest desire to be with you and my many marginal attachments that contradict your way of life. You allowed division in my family, in the circle of my friends, and among the members of my community—even within the church I belong to. Indeed, they do not feel the same way I feel about you in so many ways.

You also allowed division between me and my fellow workers, even and especially those who believe in you. Why?

Because the teachings of yours that I chose to follow seem opposite to what the majority teaches. Your truth does not follow the rules and criteria of analyzed statistics. Your truth cannot be submitted to a vote. Your truth is truth. Because you allowed a bitter division between me and those who are dearest to me, I sometimes feel so alone. Your "fire" side troubles me so much. I miss the old fireplace of my childhood. It was comforting; yours is not.

And what makes me even more uncomfortable is when I try to introduce your Eternal Word into our time and space-bound human life. It does not seem to fit the picture. This is why you used the image of fire. Before the establishment of peace, we have to get rid of everything that stands in the way of it. Fire cleanses our falsehoods and puts us on the side of truth. It purifies us and puts us on the side of God. This is the only way to end the violence in the world. This is the way to change the world.

The charming old days of the fireplace are gone. They were beautiful, but they are gone. The fire, however, remains.

Your Word, dear Lord, is the Eternal Light and Fire—the Holy Spirit in action. Allow me to be one of the vehicles of this Light, this Fire, to our world of sophisticated technologies and contradictions.

Amen.

✛

The Gift of a New Day

LORD,

Oh, how I like to get up early in the morning—as early as I possibly can! Sometimes I need to get up early because of my demanding job. Sometimes I simply need to finish what I have to finish.

Besides the numerous deadlines of our world, I feel fresh and lucid in the morning, and I can accomplish things faster and in a better manner.

Sometimes I get up early, by habit, because I can't sleep. No matter the reason, I always get up early to join the choir of birds in singing your glory, dear Lord, even though you might still be resting.

I love to wake you up and be the first to tell you "good morning!"—even before my neighbor's rooster crows.

The beginning of a new day is a marvelous gift. The serene peacefulness of the morning, the fading darkness of the morning, the sparkling dawn of the morning, the gracious calmness of the morning, the dignified stillness of the morning, the promising new day of the morning—they fascinate and inspire me. There is nothing more charming than witnessing the emerging light of each day—and watching how you, my Lord, wake up every day in every human being, every animal, and every leaf. Everything stretches and unfolds. Perhaps the best symbol of you is to experience this unfolding beauty in the morning. The Invisible is seen through the perceptible. This is a true epiphany, indeed.

I've always had a special preference for the earliest religious service of the morning. It is so special to start a new day by sharing prayer at the foot of your altar. There, beautiful concerned people gather together, hand in hand, heart to heart, to thank you for the night that just became memory and to ask you for light for the day ahead. They are there for themselves, for all those who are in their hearts and minds, and for the entire world.

Also, in the morning, for about half an hour, I indulge in doing nothing—just enjoying "being." This time is and will always be one of my most important and favorite times. It leads me to the belief that there is more to life than getting things done, that my busyness is not more important than starting a new day with you, dear Lord. That brief half hour of contemplation makes a big difference in the entire day—and all of life.

By grounding myself in your divine presence in the early hours of the morning, by taking an enjoyable deep breath, and by witnessing the wonders of the birth of a new day, I realize that things keep changing—just as everything in me keeps changing. I also realize that there is, at the same time, the constancy of the wisdom of evolution, within me and without. Everything is evolving according to your plan, dear Lord. Everything is touched by the Holy Spirit, the God of evolution and spiritual growth, who makes everything new.

Thank you, Lord, for this marvelous dawn of light, insight, possibilities, opportunities, and adventures.

Thank you for the gift of each new day.

Amen.

The Gift of a New Day

LORD,

Thank you for helping me as I keep changing. I can imagine how boring it would have been if, by my tenth birth-day, I had achieved all the knowledge and wisdom I would ever need. As it is, I have changed my mind about things—many things, many times. I am glad to have had this tremendous possibility for change, for this is how I correct my mistakes and improve my life.

Because my knowledge and understanding constantly grow, my life is richer, for I see things through the wonder of childhood, the idealism of youth, and the wisdom and maturity of adulthood. I know that my point of view has been influenced by people and things and in what context I saw them. For example, each group I've belonged to over the years has influenced me in some way: my nation, my race, my gender, my church, my business, my town. Their perspectives have influenced mine, haven't they. And the other person can be—at the same time—a friend to be cherished, an enemy to be avoided, a victim to be pitied, or a messenger of God to be truly loved. The bottom line in every situation, however, has been, "What's in it for me?"—and this is exactly where the trouble begins, for this kind of selfishness changes my vision. It turns me away from the single eye I am supposed to have, the eye that brings me into focus: your will.

When I see things only from my own point of view, contradictions naturally occur. I see things from the situation I am in at that time in that particular moment. As a result, I selfishly change with the changing of my own personal interests.

Only your will, dear Lord, keeps me in focus, and my vision of you transcends my many worldly interests. You were absolutely right when you said that I cannot serve two masters (see Matthew 6:24), for where my treasure is, there my heart is also (see Matthew 6:21).

So help me, Lord, to give up my double-mindedness and to set my heart completely upon you, with one single eye to behold you. Then let me carry this vision into my daily life. Do not let my prayer be an obstacle to reaching and seeing you—for I need to reach you, whether or not I perform my prayer "properly" by following all the rules. Let not my mind and heart and all my being be distracted from you. Never.

Let me see the world in and through my prayerful focus—with you and upon you. Then I no longer feel divided. Then I no longer need to compartmentalize my life. Then "there is no longer Jew or Greek, there is no longer slave or free, there is no longer male and female; for all . . . are one in Christ Jesus" (Galatians 3:28). Then I am free to reach out to anyone and anything, without concerns for some kind of return. Then your light, through me, becomes my true vision and the light of world.

Let me live fully an existential transcendence. Let my focus be *you*.

Amen.

LORD,

Your gospel bothers me—not just sometimes but often. Let me give you a few examples. You said: "If anyone comes to me without turning his back on his father and mother, his wife and his children, his brothers and sisters, indeed his very self, he cannot be my follower" (see Luke 14:26). "Let the dead bury their own dead; but as for you, go and proclaim the kingdom of God" (Luke 9:60). "No one who puts a hand to the plow and looks back is fit for the kingdom of God" (Luke 9:62). "Sell all that you own and distribute the money to the poor, and you will have treasure in heaven; then come, follow me" (Luke 18:22).

Your gospel bothers me because it keeps reminding me that I should never feel totally comfortable where I am, that I am supposed to be on the move all the time. Therefore the "having it together" attitude I am usually proud of must be mere illusion, false comfort, and phony settlement. We are called, it seems, to quit our familiar places and proceed to unknown territories. Yes, we are pilgrims on our faith journeys. Every time we try to settle and feel at home, we somehow miss the point of the call of the kingdom of God.

Lord,

It hurts to give up today what I was proud of yesterday. In a sense, it is confusing and disturbing. But when you chose to become one of us, you were the most displaced person who ever lived—and yet you were able to make it fine. So I am going to try to make it your way. Please help me to do it the way you did it. After all, you were in my situation. You know how to handle everything. Please help! Would you?

Like many people, I've already moved many times—from country to country, town to town, culture to culture, school to school, and job to job. I've also moved many times from idea to idea, from one way of thinking to another way of thinking, from one lifestyle to another lifestyle. For many times, what I thought was new and original became, in a short while, old-fashioned and too conservative. Customs, family, and even Church traditions that played a central role in the years of my growth are not appreciated anymore; in some cases, they're even laughed at. It seems that it is almost impossible to keep any sense of connectedness to the past, any sense of rootedness.

Displacement and a sense of loss, mixed with bitterness and resentment: This is what I often feel.

Is this what you meant, Lord, when you asked me to leave my father and mother, let the dead bury the dead, and keep my hand on the plow and not look back? If this is what you want from me, I ask you to make my displacement not a single event in my life but a state of mind and a way of life. Displace me from my old-fashioned way of seeing you in your abstract mental attributes, to seeing the living you here and now. Indeed, knowing you from books and hearsay is quite different from really experiencing you. The most beautiful concepts of you are not you. Still I don't know you if I don't have a personal, direct experience of you.

Displace me from the impression that I can be a better Christian if I know more *about* you, dear Lord, for you are not mere information. You are a passionate energy that transforms lives and makes history. Make of my life your history, too.

Displace me from my too-wordy prayers, for they can get between you and me and lead me to mere learning about you. Displace me that I might set my heart solely upon you.

Displace me from my too-worldly mentality, my concerns about what people think of me and how popular I am, my interest in all this madness about competition and rivalry, and this attitude of using, measuring, comparing, evaluating, and weighing others and things. Replace all of this with a real and genuine compassion for all your children. Being like others in their brokenness will bring me closer to you than distinction in wealth, position, and power—and this "being like others" is found in mercy and compassion.

Displace me from my fears, for I do have many of them. Like a good majority of my companions, I am afraid of losing my job, of getting sick, of failing to carry out my dreams, of succeeding in meeting what I am looking for, of boredom, of slavery, of freedom—of everything. But then I read your gospel, where you say, "It is I; do not be afraid" (see Matthew 14:27; John 6:20) and "Do not fear, only believe" (Mark 5:36). Even though it is hard to follow your teachings, I am going to follow this one literally. I want to believe in you and trust you completely. I want to get rid of my fears. Maybe then I will realize that sanctity is actually freedom from my inhibiting fears.

Lord,

All your saints—to be able to become saints—have displaced themselves voluntarily in location, time, and especially attitude. Let me do just that. I am not asking you to remove me *from* the world but to remove me *of* the world. Make of my human journey a pilgrimage to your kingdom, with my eyes set upon you.

Lord,

Keep me on the move, forward, upward—Godward. Make of the history of my life, your history.

Amen.

LORD,

Our society equates worth with money, productivity, owning, busyness, competition, action, desire to be always "on top of things," and eagerness for the new: new encounters, new events, new experiences, new managements, new cars—new anything. We seem to be too "active," even when it comes to "good and religious" works. The many programs we have concerning the hungry, the sick, the oppressed, the suffering, etc. are beautiful, even if they are never enough.

But dear Lord, let all this work be according to your calling and not just the expression of our needs and self-satisfaction. Let us be critical of our activist tendencies by yielding to your will. The salvation of the world does not depend on us but on you. Our faith, not our activism, will remove the mountains. Only then will our action be based on solid ground, therefore blessed, even though it occurs in the midst of chaos, confusion, hatred, and violence.

Lord, let us realize that "doing things" is not more important than prayer, and prayer is not something we do when nothing urgent has to be done.

Let us understand that the language we sometimes use, like "I'm too busy to pray" or "I don't have the opportunity to pray" or "Every time I decide to pray, something urgent demands all my attention," is inappropriate language. For prayer is not a waste of time, even in an impatient world filled with emergencies and urgencies. Let us always focus, before and above all, on "the one thing required" (see Luke 10:42).

Lord, make our actions be the fruit of our prayer—our intimacy with you.

Amen.

LORD,

Sometimes I dream of an ideal community—a kind of heaven on earth. I feel a deep urge to think about it, read about it, search for it, and even to try constructing it.

How many people have tried to develop ideal communities and "promised lands" where people can live in perfect conditions and in harmony? Where are these communities, dear Lord? Anywhere? Isn't this ideal phenomenon called *utopia*?

Political systems, such as socialism, communism, and democracy, have tried to develop such social utopias. Liberty, brotherhood, human rights, freedom to worship as one pleases, and equality are only a few ideas of such utopian dreams—aren't they?

Pioneers in any field, explorers of new lands, and creators of new settlements, communes, and cults are often searching for some form of utopia by trying to establish an ideal community in which everything is the way it is "supposed" to be. Founders of religious orders or charismatic movements are trying the best they can to anticipate the life of heaven here on earth—aren't they?

All these dreams are wonderful. They are highly motivating and can inspire us to do more and more, even to help the grass to become greener.

So often, however, we are disappointed. We find ourselves beginning to wonder if we might be looking in the wrong directions.

Lord,

Is the kingdom of God you talked about a utopia, too?

Is it the theological term for a dream that never comes true?

"Love one another," simplicity, responsibility, justice, integrity, innocence, sense of purpose, and all other evangelical and human values: Are these mere dreams?

Lord,

Help me to start believing that the kingdom of God that you came to initiate is not a utopia but a joyful reality here and now. It is your divine presence in everyone and in all things, at all times, even where and when you seem to be absent. Help me to understand that every time I act with loving forgiveness, compassion, and justice toward everyone I meet, I am contributing to the "thy kingdom come" and making of this earth your kingdom, your home.

Lord,

To have found you is not the end of my search or the achievement of the kingdom. It is only the beginning of the most fascinating journey on earth—to walk with you and bring you to others.

Help me to remember that with you I have the strength to do anything, including letting the dream-utopia of the kingdom of God come true.

Please, Lord, help me to do just that.

Amen.

LORD,

What do you look like?

I know that you exist.

I know that you are powerful; you made the world.

I know that you are intelligent and aesthetic; you designed the world and made of it a masterpiece of art and being.

But it seems to me that I can believe in all this and still despair, for I do not know why I am living. I need real meaning for my life. I really do.

Solomon believed in you as a faceless Being. "When I applied my mind to know wisdom, and to see the business that is done on earth, how one's eyes see sleep neither day nor night, then I saw all the work of God, that no one can find out what is happening under the sun. However much they may toil in seeking, they will not find it out; even though those who are wise claim to know, they cannot find it out" (Ecclesiastes 8:16-17).

This is, I would say, knowing you from the back—that is, knowing you from what you have done.

But who are you? What does your face look like?

Solomon did not consider himself your child; rather, you were his Unknown.

Jesus said that you are good, loving, just, that you care deeply about all of us. He gave us a new status. Now you are the Father and we are the children.

This is a huge change. Sometimes, even two thousand years after Jesus, we do not fully realize that you are our loving Father.

Jesus is the incarnation of Sonhood, love, goodness, and truth. He is the supreme image of both the nature of God and the extent of human potential. He is fully divine and fully human. To see how close you are, I look to him. To see how far I can go, I look to him. He is the perfect divine and human face. He is the way.

Jesus has identified himself with everyone.

Jesus is your face.

Everyone is supposed to be—ought to be—Jesus' face. Therefore we are your face in the Son.

Lord,

One hundred years from now, it will not matter how much wealth I accumulated, what kind of clothes I wore, or what kind of car I drove. Who cares about these things one hundred years from now? What really matters is to have made this world a little better by making a difference, in letting your face be more apparent in mine and in seeing your face in others.

Lord, help me to do just that. Only then will I know concretely what you look like. Only then will I have new meaning to my life.

✢

LORD,

Please help me to be on the side of truth. Please do not let me align myself with the majority if the majority is not on the side of truth.

Help me to see all the truth about myself. Too much selfishness makes me blind, deaf, and closed to new growth.

Help me to be true to myself. Only by being true to myself will I grow close to you and others.

Help me to speak the truth, especially before those who have the power to reject me, the ones who are approved by others and applauded, and the ones who love me and trust me.

Lord, reveal to me what I really want in life, for my wants are so fed by illusion and watered down by mirage.

Help me to avoid that inappropriate word, the indifferent glance, the icy attitude, for they are all sophisticated weapons against others. And strengthen me when others use these weapons against me.

Grant me the meekness and docility of a lamb, the intransigence and uncompromising stance of a wolf.

Teach me to forgive, for forgiveness displays strength and confidence. Vengeance only hides weakness and insecurity.

Teach me to accept myself, for then I will not be so frightened when I am asked to accept others.

Teach me, Lord, to be present to you and others, for only then can I enjoy depth in communication and intensity in being and becoming.

Teach me to be still when I want to run away, and make me fly when attachment means inertness, lifelessness, and disintegration of my soul.

Help me to see the other side of a dispute. Convince my heart of the good intentions of others, even and especially when they disagree with me.

And, Lord,

If you grant me success, do not take away my ambition to change and continually grow.

If you grant me wealth, do not deprive me of humility and happiness.

If you bestow health and well-being on me, do not let me forget my deep gratitude to you for these generous gifts.

If you count me among the powerful, do not let my sense of humility slip away from me.

If you bless me with friends, do not allow me to lose my intimacy with you and with my true self.

If you foster in me the courage of true self-esteem, do not let my wonder dissipate in erudition and judgment.

If you accord me the faculty to choose everything in life, do not let my embarrassment prevent me from discerning the one essential choice: my God.

If you give me the energy to transform the world, do not let me disavow fidelity to the One from whom this energy flows.

If, at any moment, I lose sight of you, please, Lord, keep a close watch over my impudent steps, and if I try to dawdle away and hide from your concerned eye, please, Lord, pick

Fullness of Life

me up in your arms and draw me to your heart, where I can embrace the flame of your love and feel the warmth of being at home again.

And Lord,

Make of your divine love the love, the story, and the life of my life, so I can dare to live my life—your love—to the fullest.

Amen.

LORD,

On the third day, you arose from the dead.

Your resurrection is supposed to renew the whole world. But why does this not happen at times? Don't you hear the agonizing cries of millions of people who are burdened with oppression, depression, sickness, and all kinds of brokenness? Your victory over death should make a difference in a person's life. But why do so many people remain the same as if you were still among the dead?

Lord, what is this new life your Church talks about when, on the very day of your joyous resurrection, one person loses a spouse or a child, another remains lonely and depressed, another feels unloved and becomes unable to love, another is diagnosed with an incurable disease?

We are wounded people, dear Lord. Can anyone truly believe that the gift of new life and the promise of victory over darkness are more than hopeful words? Are our prayers becoming mere wishes—maybe even hypocritical statements? Wounds are deep in our own lives. Somehow we feel them more on holidays than at any other time, maybe especially on an Easter Sunday afternoon when we become aware of our brokenness after we proclaim, "The joy of the resurrection renews the whole world."

But somehow I heard your voice saying in my depths, "I am the One, the only One, who gives life. I am the only One who loves you without limits and without conditions." Then I arose with you and my joy was complete. I am "created anew" (see Galatians 6:15). "Everything old has passed away; see, everything has become new!" (2 Corinthians 5:17).

And this was my resurrection, too.

The vision of "a new heaven and a new earth" (Revelation 21:1) takes the despair out of death, the morbidity and harm out of suffering and mishaps, and the hopelessness out of the complexity of our chaotic lives.

Our future began on the day of your resurrection. The glimpses of a new earth are seen every time a stranger is welcomed, a naked person is clothed, a sick person is visited, an oppressed soul is liberated, an old way of thinking is replaced by what you taught us.

In the new city, you are with us until the end of time. This is what your resurrection means. Then who cares about tears? Your presence in our midst wipes away every tear and "death will be no more; mourning and crying and pain will be no more, for the first things have passed away" (Revelation 21:4).

Congratulations, dear Lord! Not for you—you do not need anyone to congratulate you. Rather, congratulations for us! We are saved! Let your resurrection wipe away every tear from my eyes and from my heart.

Amen.

✛

LORD,

I believe in you + I believe that, with you, I am able to do anything + I believe that, with you, I can make it to the top = I will make it to the top.

Amen.

LORD,

    Help me to do things prayerfully.

    Help me to do things the best I can.

    Help me to do things always with you.

    Then I will "have the strength for everything" (see Philippians 4:13).

    Help me to always do things your way.

    I am sure, by doing things this way, you will do with me what you are pleased to do, and the things I'll do will be pleasing to you.

    Amen! Amen! Amen!

PART TWO

Reflections on
Prayer

Do you sometimes feel empty? I do. Even though we know that we love God and that God loves us, we still feel empty at times. It seems there is a big hole at the center of our being that needs to be filled, and we often fill it with the wrong things. No matter how much food or drink we pour in that hole, how many cars and houses we own, how much money we have in the bank, how many friends we have, how many pleasures we count on to extinguish our thirst, that hole is never filled or quenched.

John is an intelligent, independent, and self-sufficient man. He is a churchgoer and tries to do all things right. He is also well-connected with people. He has the money to buy almost anything he wants, and he has many friends. But somehow he feels lonely, even in the midst of his loving family, whom he cherishes. "I probably need nothing," John said, "for I can buy anything I want and yet, I still feel there is a big hole within me that needs to be filled."

The hole John is talking about is the deep longing for the Infinite, for God. Because we are created to be intimate with our God, this hole will keep reminding us that nothing will satisfy us totally except him. Augustine described this feeling this way: "Our hearts are restless and they will know no rest until they rest in you." The psalmist expressed it this way:

O God, you are my God, I seek you,
   my soul thirsts for you;
my flesh faints for you,
   as in a dry and weary land where
   there is no water (Psalm 63:1).

The Samaritan woman drawing water from the well said to Jesus: "Sir, give me this water, so that I may never be thirsty or have to keep coming here to draw water" (John 4:15).

It is through prayer that we find this water that is our intimacy of being with God. Prayer brings us back to this intimacy when we fall away from it. Prayer moves us closer to him who never in truth leaves us.

Intimacy with God develops a little at a time, and if we really want it, we won't miss it; we will schedule a time for it. We will consecrate a little time in the morning and in the evening, and maybe during the day. In fact, we may want to consider this advice from St. Francis de Sales: All Christians need a half hour of prayer each day, except when they are busy. Then they need an hour.

If we really want to develop a close relationship with the Lord, nothing can substitute the time we spend in each other's company. Then, little by little, we will feel we cannot leave the One who never leaves us. Then our entire life becomes invaded by his presence. Whatever we happen to be doing becomes prayer.

Nothing can extinguish our deep thirst except our closeness to God. Nothing can fill that big hole within us except our intimacy with him. This is the water that gives life. "Those who drink of the water that I will give them will never be thirsty. The water that I will give will become in them a spring of water gushing up to eternal life" (John 4:14).

"Give Me This Water"

Daily prayer, twenty-four hours every couple of months in a retreat center, keeping a personal journal where we can write letters to God to tell him all that is in our heart: These are just a few suggestions of things we can do that will nurture our intimacy with God.

Then we, too, will draw the living water Jesus was talking about.

"Give Me This Water"

In a world of cause and effect, God might seem to be the Supreme Cause of all happenings: God is the Creator and the human being is only an instrument or object in his hands, one of the effects of this First Cause. In such a case, the human being is not really free or responsible and has no individual dignity. Prayer becomes merely a means of influencing the First Cause to produce different effects.

In this paradigm, human beings pray to God to intervene and to meet their varied needs. In sickness, one uses prayer to ask God for healing. In material poverty, one uses prayer to ask God for money. In the case of a dissatisfied life, prayer is the tool used to make the person happy again. We ask God for everything and anything, including victory in war. Imagine how human beings must sometimes confuse this God! When two countries, two parties, two ideologies, or two persons are in a state of war and pray to the same God for victory, what is God going to do? Can God take sides? *Does* God take sides? Can human beings change God's mind? It is certainly legitimate to pray and ask for all these things. But deep down in our hearts and souls, we may be praying for the wrong reasons.

And how about those persons who have it all: wealth, health, fame, position, education, wisdom, a beautiful family—everything? These persons still need to pray, even though they don't seem to need anything.

But do we really need reasons to pray? When we pray, should we search for motives? Should we pray because . . . and because . . . and because? Do our prayers need to have causes, otherwise we do not need to pray? These questions are rather intellectual and theoretical, yet prayer must be seen as a spiritual activity that does not need reasons or proofs. If we really do not want to pray, if we have all the proof and reasons, if we force ourselves to say some formulas called "prayer," is this prayer?

In this sense, God does not need prayers. Let us stop this business of turning God into a king who is anxious for homage or a superpower who, when asked, is pleased to grant health, wealth, jobs, positions, successful elections, and whatever else comes to mind. In prayer, it is not God who has to change; rather, we are the ones who change. Prayer is a faithful surrender to God, letting him do whatever he has wanted to do for a long time but we would not allow it. Very often—maybe most of the time—we do not have the same ideas and opinions that God has. Yet, God knows better than we do what is good for us. We pray that we might be "participants of the divine nature" (2 Peter 1:4), to be divinized in trustful surrender to his will.

In the scientific world in which we live, causality does not have the same meaning it once had. There is no longer a "final cause," and God is no longer seen this way. Rather, God created us as responsible people and means his creation to be responsible. So when we pray, we immediately begin to work for what we are praying. It is true that God provides food for the birds, but it is also true that God does not send his angels to put food in the birds' nests. He did better than this; he gave birds their wings and vital energy to go out and find the food they need at the moment they need it.

Why Do We Pray?

It is absurd for human beings to pray in a passive way. God gave us the power to participate in his work—and this is exactly what we should do when we pray. In fact, when we pray, God prays in us; when we act, God acts through us. In prayer, we are changed over and over. Our hearts are more important vessels for change than are our ideological, social, and political systems. We alone, however, cannot change our hearts; rather, in prayer, God helps us begin to see things the way he sees them, and act the way he acts. In prayer, we are dislodged from our usual comfortable habits, from what is familiar, from a sense of grief for our old selves, from a fear of all that is new. In prayer, we deepen our sense of responsibility for others; we grow closer to others and others become more a part of ourselves. Prayer, then, leads us necessarily to action.

Why Do We Pray?

We all do things for reasons. Right? Don't we expect, at least in the back of our minds, to receive some profit from any activity we undertake? But profit is not only material; it can be physical, emotional, and spiritual as well.

Fran is a rich lady. Besides a chain of hotels, she owns stocks with airlines and computer companies. She also is a fervent churchgoer. Every year Fran gives a large sum of money to charity and deducts this money from her taxes. She feels better about herself for having made a contribution and believes that someday she will be rewarded in heaven because she helped God's poor.

Nothing for nothing. This is how our culture compels the majority of us to be.

So what is the payoff of prayer? Does it really pay to pray, even if we know that we are unable to change God's mind?

Peter is a man of prayer. He also worships at the altar of his family. He is proud of his family, enjoys time with each member of his family, and prays every day for his family. He thinks he is lucky to have an "ideal" Christian family. One day, however, this ideal failed when a question of inheritance created enmity between himself and his brothers and sisters. Peter became almost paralyzed by guilt, not because he did anything wrong but because he felt that he did not do enough to prevent this conflict. He decided to remain on the side of integrity and justice—which meant he had to be tough, not so "likable." People—even family members—are bothered by persons of integrity. In this situation, Peter prayed and prayed and prayed, not that he might receive his share of the inheritance but that he might contribute to recreating the "ideal" Christian family as it is supposed to be: unified. He wanted a prayerful relationship for and with his family. He wanted to see the gospel not as a mere resource of knowledge but as a healing word for the present moment. For Peter, this conflict continues.

Why, then, does Peter pray? Why do you pray? Why do I pray?

Perhaps we pray because we have nothing to lose—and maybe, someday, much to gain here and beyond. Perhaps we pray because we believe that prayer can help bring us prosperity, health, and general well-being. After all, human beings once believed that prosperity was a sign of God's blessing. Perhaps we pray because we want to insure our one-way ticket to heaven. Perhaps we pray for many other reasons as well.

In reality, we pray to be in the presence of God, right now, right here. Spiritual masters talk about the "sacrament of the present moment." This is exactly what prayer is: to live in the presence of God anytime, anyplace.

Yet, the presence of God may not have practical utility. In fact, the presence of God could be, practically speaking, harmful. Peter, for example, is financially damaging himself with the stand he is taking on the inheritance conflict. With his integrity and prayerful lifestyle, he cannot make money; he cannot even receive the money due to him. Yet, Peter continues to pray for himself and his entire family. Why? Because he wants to develop in himself and in the world around him an atmosphere of peace, faith, and love. From a

Does It Pay to Pray?

financial point of view, this is not a good investment on Wall Street. But this is what Peter feels he needs to do because Paul's voice does not leave his mind: "Do not be conformed to this world, but be transformed by the renewing of your minds, so that you may discern what is the will of God—what is good and acceptable and perfect" (Romans 12:2). For Peter, Christ is not merely some kind of energy for a happier future; rather, Christ is as an essential living element that Peter relies on as he tries to make heaven a part of his life here and now. Peter is not trying to earn points for heaven, so to speak. Rather, he wants to develop a sense of living holiness by sanctifying the present "messy" moment he is in.

A happy ending, then, is always in sight. Maybe it will not be a happy ending in a material sense, but it will certainly be a "spiritual" happy ending. Peter is transforming his bad situation into an opportunity to practice the presence of God for himself and his family in truth.

Does it pay to pray? Of course it does. Prayer trains the heart's eyes to see the "beyond" in all the twists and corners of life. Prayer brings us Christ's gifts of faith, love, and peace, no matter the situation. It is working for Peter, for he is able to involve God in his difficult situation. It will work for you and me as well. When we focus on the "beyond," the details of life appear somehow secondary—and they are.

Does It Pay to Pray?

We should pray without ceasing and without interruption. Prayer is not only that period of time that we spend with God. Rather, prayer is our life, the life we live, day and night, in joy and in sorrow, when we are in need and when we are in prosperity, at work and at play, without interruptions and breaks—even when we are on our coffee break.

Jesus asks for this unceasing prayer. "Jesus told them a parable about their need to pray always and not to lose heart" (Luke 18:1). "Pray constantly" (see Luke 21:36). And even though Jesus does not describe in great detail how to pray, he does give his disciples some guidelines to follow (see Matthew 6:5-8) and teaches them the Lord's Prayer (see Matthew 6:9-13; Luke 11:2-4). Notice that the Lord's Prayer is introduced by Jesus at the request of the disciples: "Lord, teach us to pray" (Luke 11:1). Jesus, no doubt, uses this very prayer himself when he slips away to pray quietly. And in paying close attention to Jesus at prayer (see Matthew 26:36-44; Mark 1:35-36, 6:31-32; Luke 3:21, 5:16, 9:18, 28, 11:1-2, 22:32, 39-45; John 17), we cannot miss noticing that his prayers are for more closeness with the Father, clearer discernment of the Way, and more dynamic action. Jesus never says to his disciples to just read, study, reflect, meditate, and contemplate. Rather, he tells them to give, feed, seek, heal, sow, build, go, do: "Not everyone who says to me, 'Lord, Lord,' will enter the kingdom of heaven, but only the one who does the will of my father in heaven" (Matthew 7:21). Prayer is a continuous state of reflection and action. This is apparent in the mind, heart, and life of Jesus.

Saint Paul is explicit on this point as well. "Pray without ceasing, give thanks in all circumstances; for this is the will of God in Christ Jesus for you" (1 Thessalonians 5:17–18). "We always pray for you, asking that our God will make you worthy of his call" (2 Thessalonians 1:11). "Be filled with the Spirit . . . giving thanks to God the Father at all times and for everything in the name of our Lord Jesus Christ" (Ephesians 5:18, 20). "Persevere in prayer" (Romans 12:12). "Devote yourselves to prayer, keeping alert in it with thanksgiving" (Colossians 4:2). "Pray in the Spirit at all times in every prayer and supplication" (Ephesians 6:18). "In our prayers for you we always thank God, the Father of our Lord Jesus Christ" (Colossians 1:3). "I am grateful to God . . . when I remember you constantly in my prayers night and day" (2 Timothy 1:3). "I remember you always in my prayers" (Romans 1:9). "Whether you eat or drink, or whatever you do, do everything for the glory of God" (1 Corinthians 10:31). "Whatever you do, in word or deed, do everything in the name of the Lord Jesus, giving thanks to God the Father through him" (Colossians 3:17).

This insistence on unceasing prayer should not be seen as a *part* of living; rather, it is *all* of living. This prayer should include our thoughts, emotions, feelings, words, actions—all our beings. It is obvious that unceasing prayer, whose champion is Paul, does not mean that we should be in church day and night or at least thinking of God twenty-four hours a day. This is an unrealistic quest, even for monks and nuns. Such activity would only expose one to a mental breakdown.

Rather, living unceasing prayer means to live our ordinary lives in the presence of God, in a constant state of contemplation, joy, and celebration. We do not have to divide life into segments—thoughts and feelings for God and thoughts and feelings for God's world. No! We are to do whatever we do, at all times, in the presence and love of God. Then the entire quality of our thoughts, feelings, and actions will change and become continuous prayer.

Jesus lived his life in the presence of his Father. He shared his joys, his fears, his hopes, and his despairs with the Father. "I am not alone because the Father is with me" (John 16:32). Jesus did not hide anything from the Father—and neither should we. Prayer is the right tool by which we join all of our spiritual, mental, emotional, and physical processes with all of our joys, worries, and preoccupations, and direct them toward God in the confident trust that everything, through his generous grace, will become a hymn to his glory.

Richard has a full life. He must provide for his family and has a demanding job. He also likes to have fun with his friends. He likes to eat good food, play tennis and chess, swim, and read. For Richard, twenty-four hours a day is not enough time to do all that he wants to do. In anything he happens to be doing, however, he focuses on God. He lets the Lord be involved totally in his life. He never does what he does alone; rather, he does everything with God. He takes time to notice events, objects, and persons, and he notes their effects on him. He listens to what God is telling him through these events, objects, and persons—the struggles, the

suffering, and the incredible joy. Richard knows that our
world cannot be perfect. He knows, too, that God communi-
cates through the imperfect reality of all that we have and are.
He prays always to see the holy in what we really are as
children of God.

Unceasing prayer is an uninterrupted awareness of the
presence of God in our lives, a transformation of all our
actions into prayers. Unceasing prayer is to meet God in
the ordinary—always.

There are times in life when everything seems blooming and rosy. Our sense of closeness to God's presence at times like this is clear and comforting. All our prayers are answered, it seems, almost the way we wished. It is heaven on earth.

But can these times last forever? No. Things change. We change. Bad times invade our bodies, hearts, minds, and souls. At times like this, God seems no longer to listen to us. This, then, seems more like hell on earth.

Carol is known for her righteousness, integrity, and total dedication to her church, her husband, and her children. She found great delight in her close relationship to her God and her family. We might expect therefore that Carol would be rewarded for her total dedication. But guess what. One of her children was diagnosed with a terminal illness at the age of twenty-four. Imagine the heartbreak! God seems to have turned a deaf ear to Carol's prayers.

Jesus tells us that we will have to carry the cross, but who likes to hear about the cross? We want to make of God the guarantor of our success, wealth, health, and personal fulfillment. When we pray, we ask God to be on our side, to make nice things happen to us. But Jesus promises the cross.

Hard times, however, are important; they can be times of profound spiritual growth and insight into our lives and our relationship with our God. Until the false image of God as a "nice guy" God (like the golden calf of long ago) leaves us totally, there is no room for the real God.

During our most difficult times, it seems to us that the God we believed in is not there—really not there. As long as things are fine, we do not have the opportunity to become aware of how distorted our conceptions of God really are. Only when we die to these false conceptions of God can we experiences the real "I AM WHO I AM" (Exodus 3:14).

Carol must have experienced dryness, sadness, dissatisfaction, and disbelief, much as the ancient Hebrews felt as they went through the desert. Jesus, too, has his ordeal of crucifixion. But this is how new visions and growth come into being. Beyond darkness and death is the light and resurrection. Grace invades us when we are in great pain, when we walk through the dark valley of meaninglessness, weakness, and loss of reason for living. It invades us when despair destroys our joy and courage.

Carol continued to pray and asked her family and friends to pray as well. She persevered, persisted, insisted, and was faithful. More than ever, she stayed at the side of her God. Carol understood that to be a Christian means not only performing some religious act but also participating in the suffering of God in the life of the world. Her prayer allowed her to penetrate reality to reach her God. She prayed: "My God, my God, why have you forsaken me? Lord, I am tired and frustrated. I put my whole story into your hands. Do something about it. I cannot tell my son what the doctor told me. He will lose hope. He won't have a chance for living. Only you can see my deep concern and worry. So I pray and offer you my concern and worry. This is what I have now. Please save my son, if you choose to." Her son was saved.

It is not bad to complain to God—Job did it. He wanted explanations for his long sufferings. Even if we do not understand—and we certainly may not—our faithful prayer will give us the right vision of God. At the lowest level of sadness, we can be close to God when we drop the God of our own ideas for the real God. Ironically, we might become closer precisely when it seems God is not listening.

To be closer to God is what true prayer is about. This, too, is what real Christianity is about. Prayer is not a withdrawal from the world; rather, it is a penetration through the world to God in all the happy and sad events of our lives. Because God is the depth and meaning of what is happening to us, the real question is not whether or not we are comfortable but whether or not we have a new life, God's life. Prayer, in good and bad times, introduces us to this new life.

God listens to us but very often we do not listen to God. We can train ourselves to be ready when God speaks, however, with Samuel's prayer: "Speak, Lord, for your servant is listening" (1 Samuel 3:9).

✛

It is dangerous to pray, for praying involves change. For this reason, it is easier to go to church, say some "programmed" words, perform some rituals, and remain the same.

In our daily living, we usually are pulled by two opposite poles that can paralyzed us into indecision, leaving us not knowing which direction to go or what to do. On the one hand, there is all that we are afraid to abandon: the memories, the familiar, the comfortable, and the weight of the past. On the other hand, there is the land of hope, expectations, newness, and uncertainty that we are afraid to explore. We're also perhaps bothered by what we wanted to change and didn't, and by what we didn't want to change and did. In the midst of it all, we find ourselves weak, stubborn, shy—afraid to face the truth that we simply have not become what we're supposed to be. Perhaps we've acquired some gray hair by now, some wrinkles, some extra pounds, some failure here and there—and we cannot go back to what we were before. We are afraid of what hasn't happened—yet we are afraid of what has happened. We are invaded by fear despite Jesus' reassurance, "Do not be afraid" (Luke 12:32), for "I am the first and the last" (Revelation 1:17).

I used to go to Paris at least once a year. In 1989, I decided to break my routine and go, instead, to California. This was a dream visit that I had harbored for a long time. When my hosts in Santa Cruz picked me up at the San Jose airport, everything was fine and warm until we got to their home. Then, while we were still in our preliminary conversations,

I saw the tables and chairs beginning to sway and dishes falling to the floor—and we hurried to the nearest parking lot. This huge earthquake, with its many aftershocks, forced us to spend two nights in the car.

This was a scary experience. Survival was all that was important to us during that time; everything else was secondary. Personally, all my dreams, projects, even my conceptions were put to the test that day. I suddenly realized how transient they actually are—and yet we are not to live in fear! So I prayed, and with my prayer, fear somehow started to disappear. I found myself ready to go whenever and wherever God wanted me to go on that trip—and also in my faith journey of life.

Prayer helps us to uproot our fears. In the presence of God, worries dissipate. The grace of God transforms us.

Prayer helps us overcome our setbacks, regressions, frustrations, and discouragements, and keeps us from falling back into old patterns. Perhaps we feel some unexplained anger, fear, loneliness, or resentment; only God's unconditional love can heal these unresolved areas in our consciousness and subconscious. Prayer undermines such negative emotions and replaces them with positive ones.

Prayer helps us convert our abidance by the laws and commands to an intimate living relationship with our Lord. "Abide in me as I abide in you . . . Those who abide in me and I in them bear much fruit, because apart from me you can do nothing" (John 15:4-5). It is not by squeezing or stretching a grain that it grows; rather, a grain grows by its connection to the source of life. In the same way, we cannot grow without our connection to the Lord, who is our way and our life and our truth (see John 14:6).

Prayer helps us to bear the responsibility of becoming who we really are—the persons God has in mind. This means that we have to die to whatever blocks us from transforming love: illusions, pretensions, arrogance, possessiveness, carelessness, egotism—anything that separates us from others.

Prayer helps us identify with our special calling, our deepest longing, that which is deeper than what we do for a living, what we own, what positions we have secured—the very way we live our lives. A calling gives meaning to all of this.

Prayer may not grant us what we ask for, but it transforms us at our deepest spiritual level. It connects us with the very Source of life, which often means that the quality of our entire life will be different. Our faith is not just a weekend obligation; rather, prayer makes our faith a reality to be practiced daily in our homes, schools, streets, factories—wherever we are at anytime.

Prayer helps us to become more fully human. That old form of spirituality, which teaches the denial of our humanness and our unique identities, is becoming more and more obsolete. God is interested in you and me, as we are. This is what the Incarnation is all about.

Dare to pray. Dare to allow a new you—and therefore a new earth—to emerge. "From all your idols I will cleanse you. A new heart I will give you, and a new spirit I will put within you; I will remove from your body the heart of stone and give you a heart of flesh" (Ezekiel 36:25-26). "A new creation is everything" (Galatians 6:15). "We will all be changed" (1 Corinthians 15:51). "See, I am making all things new" (Revelation 21:5). "The Father will give you whatever you ask him in my name" (John 15:16).

Prayer transforms us. It allows God to be more involved in any circumstance of our lives. Prayer makes us the persons God calls us to be in the world. It helps us to be not what we are not, but fully what we are. God wants us to allow him to penetrate into those areas of our lives we like to keep only for ourselves. There he will surprise us as we discover that we are in his image.

Prayer transforms the world through our own transformations in God.

We usually pray for security purposes. We pray to obtain something we need, to be more in control of a situation, or to insure our place in heaven. Our culture pushes us in this direction of thinking, of course. It seems that everyone looks for more security at all levels: personal, economic, national, within and without. The bold truth is, however, that we should pray to become more vulnerable.

God boldly entered our world in the vulnerability of a newborn child—and throughout his entire life, he never lost this vulnerability. Jesus dealt vulnerably with Romans, Canaanites, Samaritans, the diseased, the demonics, the lepers, and the infectious. He then vulnerably accepted the killing wounds and forgave all those who condemned him. In a crystal-clear way, he expressed the truth about God's inner nature: It is compassionate love that gives birth to a new creation. In Christ, God became vulnerable to all of life's pains. He had to bear hurts and rejections, even from his own people. He identified himself with the needy, the poor, the outsiders, the sick. He was vulnerable.

To be vulnerable does not mean to be weak, subject to others' total influence and control, unable to stand for anything as an individual. Rather, to be vulnerable means to have a fundamental openness to be affected by others, events, life itself. It is part of being embodied, incarnate, human.

To be vulnerable means to be open to God's love, to be touched and moved by God's love, and to experience this love in one's own life.

Vulnerability enables us to enter into interpersonal communication with others on a new level, in real communion—in spite of, or maybe because of, our fragility.

Vulnerability requires courage, integrity, and strength, and enables us to overcome avoidance, denial, and frustrations. As vulnerable persons, we are ready to lose ourselves in order to find our true selves. When we are vulnerable to a lonely and suffering person, for example, that broken person somehow reveals to us what we did not know before—and we become healed.

Vulnerability means trusting God totally, counting on God's providential love, as Jesus did: "Foxes have holes, and birds of the air have nests; but the Son of Man has nowhere to lay his head" (Matthew 8:20). Dare to trust when God is leading you, even without knowing where you are being led, even if you are burdened by great suffering. Trust that through both your joys and your sufferings, God will move you in new paths and unexpected patterns, encouraging you to take new steps with a new heart.

Vulnerability means a genuine openness to others, not only to those who love and respect us, but especially to those who are "different" and do not approve of us. A willingness to share our opinions, feelings, and experiences with these people is a sign of true vulnerability. And then to forgive them. "Father, forgive them; for they do not know what they are doing" (Luke 23:34). "Be merciful, as your Father is merciful" (Luke 6:36). "Forgive, and you shall be forgiven" (Luke 6:37).

On Being Vulnerable

Anthony knows himself, in his strength as well as in his weakness. He also knows that God loves him. He does not pretend to be what he is not. Rather, he tries to empty himself of greed and selfishness to allow his Lord to come within and dwell. He makes himself ready to accept life as it is planned for him by God. He experiences joy, much joy, but also failure, depression, sadness, confusion, disappointments, and many rejections. He is hurt but for him, only the wounded can really heal. This makes his vulnerability a human journey of the heart. This is the longest and hardest journey of all, but it is also an ecstatic journey.

Prayer does not necessarily require an utterance of words. Our vulnerability to the Lord is a silent and true prayer. This most intimate interaction with the Lord is, in fact, what real prayer is about. In real payer we can afford to risk our so-called security in the midst of the events that boggle and baffle our lives, for his way is the Way—and our way as well.

Nothing is more secure than this vulnerability with the Lord. This is our most intimate prayer.

✣

On Being Vulnerable

Prayer is, above all, a genuine encounter with the Lord. It is a true relationship.

A true relationship can be scary, of course. One can be afraid to fail in a relationship because of the terrible fear of possible rejection. We can also be afraid to succeed because of the many changes we must make to adapt and adjust to the new "we" situation.

Prayer is a "You-I" relationship. You live the divine presence of the Lord in your life, here and now. Feeling his love flowing in you with every breath, you experience deep spiritual joy and comfort. You are in union and communion, and there simply are no words to describe the ecstatic state you experience. Fortunately, you do not need to make a speech to express these overwhelming feelings to God. Simple phrases like "My Lord and my God" or "My shepherd" or "I love you so much" or whatever comes spontaneously into your mind will be sufficient.

This is when you drop your masks and become an open book. You put all your cards on the table, so to speak, and you do not pretend to be anything that you are not. You say all that is in your mind, knowing that God does not censure your prayers. He is concerned about anything and everything that concerns you, loving you as you are—so be what you are. Be true to yourself. Drop your masks and false pretensions of self—they don't work with God anyway. Rather, let God reach into every area of your life, especially those areas you want to keep for yourself. Don't say, "Lord, make me holy, but not yet." Rather, say, "Lord, make me holy, for I cannot do it alone.

Your agenda, Lord, not mine." Yield to him the control of your relationship with him. Let your entire life be a joint project with him. In the process, you will learn more about God—and yourself.

Next, you find yourself falling to your knees and giving thanks. You begin to see unimagined horizons developing before your very eyes. The familiar becomes illuminated by new lights, and the routine of everyday life becomes meaningful. Holiness becomes not a distant dream but a present reality at the command of your fingertips, right here, right now.

Then you listen—listen to what the Lord is communicating to you through the book you might be reading, through the silence of the moment, through the ecstasy of the communion. The deepest communication is when we understand what the other is *not* saying. The language of love is total presence, total trust, and total surrender in honesty, integrity, openness, and fidelity; words are not necessary in the language of love.

Then you trust—trust that your beloved Lord will take care of you. You do not worry, for you know that even the birds of the air are fed. You do not count on your own wealth, fame, name, or any other earthly treasure. These are heavy bondage, whereas the Lord has no heaviness. Dependence on God is independence—real freedom. Such total trust frees you from the shackles of your so-called ordered, controlled, "peaceful" compromises with the hidden evils of unjust institutions and unfair social behaviors.

The Prayer Relationship

Such trust enables you to be the person God calls you to be in his world.

Then you practice—practice and practice and practice, for you cannot have an instant relationship with God. "Instant," after all, does not satisfy like the real thing. An in-depth and meaningful relationship must have a history consisting of shared joy, anguish, caring and being cared for, openness, honesty, removing masks, explorations: a "we" understanding instead of an "I" demand. All this takes time and much practice, and no amount of time spent to build the momentum for a satisfying relationship is wasted. Prayer is not meant to be a means for immediate gratification.

Prayer brings an end to isolation. It is the sharing of your daily life with Someone who is already alive in your heart. Prayer makes you aware of your intimacy with the God who simply does not want to leave you alone.

Relating is essential in a person's life. In fact, it can become a truly existential question of survival. You are what you love. In the prayer relationship, God is met at the center, heart to heart, person to person, being to being. To relate to God in any other way than a loving relationship is to relate to an idol, one you do not know.

The prayer relationship is a great challenge, of course. Because you keep back nothing from God, the prayer rela-tionship puts you at risk—the risk that you might lose yourself. Yet, this is precisely how you find your true self.

✛

By being who and what we really are, we give glory to God. We may say a few words, perhaps, but we don't need to. We may have some image in our head, but we don't need one. We simply are who we are: children of God. To be a child of God is to live in a certain way. This is truly prayer, existential prayer.

Existential prayer is different from essential prayer. Essential prayer is more interested in what God *is* and less interested in the *fact* that God is. Essential prayer focuses on *what* you are, rather than on the *fact* that you are. In essential prayer, you might choose to reflect on God's attributes: his mercy, for example, or his goodness, his forgiveness, his compassion, his love. For this purpose, the words of Scripture or some other words can be helpful.

In existential prayer, however, you don't need words or thoughts. Rather, you need emptiness, nothingness, and mere being—being in a state of unconditional and unrestricted love. This is a prayer of being in the presence of the Lord, in love with the Lord. This is a prayer of complete awareness. Saint John of the Cross calls it the "living flame of love." And it is, indeed, a flame—the flame of the Holy Spirit at work in you.

In existential prayer, you enjoy a certain "wisdom" (*Sophia* in Greek and *Sapientia* in Latin) that is special for the state of being in love. This wisdom is not conceptual, and it is not the result of scholarly research. It is not an intellectual event. Rather, this wisdom is imageless and supraconceptual. It is "seeing" with the eyes of love. It is, in fact, the wisdom of universal love. Some of the ancient authors called this the "state of unknowing," "blindness," and "nakedness," meaning that it is not clothed with thoughts, images, or words. In existential prayer, you sit, do nothing, and accomplish much. You accomplish a loving union with God.

Mary Magdalene sat at the feet of Jesus. Her love was so deep that she needed no words, concepts, speculations, or even thinking; she was in a state of loving self-forgetfulness. She knew an awesome silence and a deep awareness of the presence of God.

In existential prayer you become your true self, where God is the ground of your very being. There, in that fullness of being, you fully exist for you are united with God. You experience God, live God, enjoy God. You don't ask questions; you don't think. Rather, you move to the area of loving, feeling, sensing, and "seeing" with the eyes of the heart. Your prayer becomes a transforming power for living, knowingly and, most likely, unknowingly.

People usually think that effort and achievement are more important than just being. Wrong! How beautiful it is to practice the art of just being, even if we have many things to do! And how difficult this is! The greatest question ever raised remains: "To be or not to be." Indeed, it is easier to follow laws, regulations, and rituals—to do things to please God—than it is to be vulnerable to his love, to be in his loving presence. After all, with external deeds, we tend to feel safe against God. Whereas at his feet, we are touched by him, moved by him, and deeply affected by him. There at his feet, everything is transformed, for we begin to see things through the eyes of God.

Existential prayer is the most dynamic energy for changing the world. It enhances human potentials and stimulates creativity. The more we pray, the more we think and love and act like Christ. In existential prayer, we not only invite Christ to live within us, but he invites us to live in him. The reality is that in Christ, we are not lost but found, for Christ is the heart of our hearts, the power of our powers, and the life of all life. He adjusts the different notes of life—our challenges, difficulties, sadness, joys, and celebrations—and makes of them a harmonious symphony. He is totally immersed in our individual lives. In him we are our true selves. Our real identity is found in this vital and living relationship, for "in him we live and move and have our being" (Acts 17:28).

For Lao Tzu, the most difficult thing to do is to be. How often we become so busy with doing and getting that we have no time left to just be. Being, not wanting, wishing, having, and doing, is what makes prayer genuine, true, and existential.

It is probably safe to say that we often think of God as a miracle worker, the one who magically transforms war into peace, the one who makes those who are paralyzed suddenly able to walk, the one who can change people who are insane into people who are sane, the one who offers homes to the homeless and jobs to the jobless—the one who makes all things right. Didn't we learn this in school and from our culture? So we expect to be ready for a miracle from God, any needed miracle, whenever we find ourselves in difficulty. If this is true, then why doesn't this supernatural miracle worker perform miracles when he is asked to change this or that evil into good and grace? Why does he allow terrible things to happen to his innocent children? Why are there bad things happening to good people? When God is presented as a fixer—the universal fixer—it becomes much easier to understand why sick persons start to pray hard, very hard, to the point of becoming religious addicts. When these persons do not realize healing, they often become bitter and angry at God and with their religion.

God can also be seen as a "weapon" against all those who do not believe in him. Who would dare to not take sides with God? Surely threats of rejection, punishment, and abandonment can force others to the required belief system. Prayer, in this case, becomes a "God weapon" against our adversary, a means of power and control.

God and religion can also be something we turn to when we feel discomfort with ourselves, our relationships, or our world. We can use God, the Church, or a minister of the

Church as a means to escape our own discomfort. Turning to God and religion, we will feel better, accepted, praised, respected, and powerful. In this case, prayer makes us feel more comfortable wherever a certain discomfort arises.

God can also be seen as an angry God. This God is ready to punish us with sickness and disaster if we break the rules. This God is going to "get you!" Because we feel fear, guilt, shame, and bitterness in relationship with this God, our prayer becomes a means to appease his anger and so escape emotional pain.

In a materialistic society such as ours, people usually measure their self-worth by how much they earn and how much they possess. It stands to reason, then, that the way to be appreciated in this culture is to give money. This is why getting or giving money in the name of God will be a noble purpose. Prayer, at that time, will become a means to raising more money. God and prayer become just another product— and often a very good business.

Religion can also become the "opium of the people." As such, prayer is used to invoke the name of God for all the wrong reasons. God becomes the means that helps us win an election, justify a social or economic system, and maintain the privileges of a certain race, gender, class, or political party. God becomes the status quo, and prayer becomes the vehicle for ideological programs, political gain, and self-interest fanaticism.

But is this who our God is? Is our God really an angry, unforgiving, egotistic, bloody tyrant who must be feared?

Who Is This God to Whom We Pray?

Might he be a loving, accepting, joyful God, always ready to help, always life-giving, always creative? After all, he is the one who said: "Can a woman forget her nursing child, or show no compassion for the child of her womb? Even these may forget, yet I will not forget you" (Isaiah 49:15). He is the one who said: "I have loved you with an everlasting love" (Jeremiah 31:3). And it is he who "so loved the world that he gave his only Son, so that everyone who believes in him may not perish but may have eternal life" (John 3:16).

These are important questions we must face when we want to understand all there is about prayer. For prayer will not be the same in both cases. A dysfunctional sense of God, for example, provokes a dysfunctional prayer. We usually consider God as being made in our image when, actually, he is much better than we think he is. It is time to say goodbye to the magical God of our quick-fix mentality and welcome the loving God who asks us to be involved in the change we want to make in ourselves and the world.

✧

We do things the way we are—and our praying is no different. We pray as we are.

The psychology books are helpful here. Let's review how these books classify the different types of temperaments and how each type of temperament reacts to any given situation.

People of the *thinking type*—those who are rational and logical—are not usually comfortable dealing with feelings. Those of the *feeling type*—those whose hearts rather than their minds are in command—do not usually follow the law of evidence. Those of the *perceiving type*—those who are usually open-minded and receptive to new data—hate to make decisions they cannot alter later on. Those of the *judging type*— those who like order and punctuality—tend to be rigid because they know exactly what they want. Those of the *intuitive type*—those who are imaginative and insightful—look to see what is ahead. Those of the *sensing type*—those who are down-to-earth and trust facts not theories and abstractions— want to enjoy the now rather than defer enjoyment to a future time. Those of the *introvert type*—those who are private and independent—are interested mainly in the inner life. Those of the *extrovert type*—those who are bored when they're by themselves—get their energy for living from others.

The descriptions of these major personality types are, of course, oversimplified; the reality is much more complex. It is rare, in fact, for a person to be associated with only one type. My intention here is not the study of personality types but to show that our prayer is affected by our dominant type of personality.

Each personality type has its own preference for prayer, which explains why there are so many paths for prayer. The kind of prayer that works for James, for example, may not work for Carol. No wonder we have Trinitarian spirituality, the spirituality of the Desert Fathers and Mothers, Benedictine spirituality, Augustinian spirituality, Franciscan spirituality, Thomistic spirituality, Ignatian spirituality, Teresian spirituality, and others—and thus different types of prayers. For example, there is the prayer of the feeling function, the prayer of the thinking function, the prayer of the sensing function, and the prayer of the intuitive function. There also is the prayer of the introvert and the prayer of the extrovert. Each is a way of praying, but each is different. If you tell me how you pray, I'll tell you who you are.

There is a different type of prayer for each type of personality. Studies and experiences point to a close relationship between an innate temperament and the type of prayer that is suitable to our needs. It is probably safe to say that there is no "best" type of prayer that is suitable for everyone. Without denying the value and spiritual riches of other types of prayer, it is safe to say that what works for you is best for you.

Keep in mind, however, that God can and does intervene in our lives in his own way. Thus, do not be frustrated if you see that a certain type of prayer that works for your friend does not work effectively for you. By knowing yourself, you will know what kind of prayer is suitable for you.

God loves you as you are, the way he created you. God wants you to be yourself, not somebody else.

Every way that leads to God is good. Find the way that works best for you.

✣

When prayer becomes our way of being, it makes history. When prayer becomes a living love, the entire world changes, for living love is the most dynamic and transforming form of prayer.

When the human heart is changed—which is the hardest part—systems change as a natural effect. By changing the human heart, prayer affects our systems, becomes hope and action, and produces the future. Prayer causes action and action makes the kingdom come. Prayer and action do not contradict each other; rather, they complement each other. They are, at the level of holiness, transformed into one entity: love. "Thy kingdom come" is not only a prayer; it is a program of action.

Mother Teresa of Calcutta is an incarnate example of prayer and action. This woman, who earned the admiration of the entire world, says, "The value of our actions corresponds exactly to the value of the prayer we make, and our actions are fruitful only if they are the true expression of earnest prayer." She also says, "Active and contemplative are not two different lives; it is only that one is faith in action through service, the other faith in action through prayer."

Charles de Foucauld did not preach revolution in North Africa, even though he wasn't happy with the Europeans who did not show respect for the original inhabitants of the region. Rather, he looked after the sick; he cooked for them, cleaned their wounds, and helped to fight general starvation. At the same time, he recognized that what he was doing couldn't be sustained unless prayer remained a constant source of strength and inspiration for him. From Charles we learn that the greater our commitment is to action the more we are in need of prayer and union with God.

It has been said that St. Teresa of Avila wanted one day to build a large orphanage but she did not have more than three shillings. People asked her how she could start such a project with so little money. Teresa laughed and said: "Teresa can do nothing with three shillings, but with three shillings plus God, nothing is impossible."

Prayer and action are not mutually exclusive. In fact, prayer without action can be hypocritical pietism—and action without prayer can be hollow activism. True prayer compels us to engage fully in concrete acts of service, which cannot be genuinely pursued without prayer that brings help from above. Prayer inspires us to see things the way God sees them, and helps us to act accordingly.

God's grace transforms our every thought, feeling, word, and action. The Spirit enables us to do what we are supposed to do. If I am a teacher, for example, the Spirit will provide me the ability to understand and assist my individual students in many different ways. If I am a writer, the Spirit will help me bridge the gap between the creative inspiration of my writing and the "rhetorical" style of it. If I am a factory worker, the Spirit will pull me toward a more insightful atti-tude regarding my repetitive assembly-line tasks. In prayer, the Spirit will tell me how to be closer to others, how to do my immediate job better, and how to follow my special calling and my lifelong vocation using all the gifts he has given me.

On Prayer and Action

When we cooperate so intimately with God's grace, letting the divine energy inflame our own energies, we enter into the process of the total integration of the body-soul-heart-mind-earth-God, which is the process of divinization, the final goal of every human being. This is a continuous global growth through the daily prayer action of our extraordinary, ordinary lives, until we become other Christs.

How rare is silence in our lives today! We seem to have a need for continuous noise. If it is not talking or crying or laughing, it is radio, telephone, or television. Somehow we fear to expose ourselves to silence, for we don't know what will surface from within when the external noise is eliminated. Some of us cannot even fall asleep in a quiet environment.

Sound or noise seems to reassure us; it allows us to escape from ourselves into a distraction. Silence, on the other hand, scares us. We fear we will be exposed to the sound of our own voice—something we really don't want to hear. Also, we may hear more clearly God's voice speaking to us—something we prefer not to deal with.

Silence, however, must be a timeless treasure, for in Christian history men and women sought it eagerly. Jesus himself would withdraw to pray in the silence of a quiet place. Before starting his ministry, for example, he went out into the desert by himself, seeking complete silence. Through the years, silence has been cherished by all the saints, for in silence they have felt more united with God. Some religious orders have actually established "silence" as a requirement, and "breaking the great silence" was considered a big mistake, if not a sin.

Silence, for me personally, is an important part of my life. In silence I hear what God is trying to tell me—much more so than in the events of my life. In silence I can be more deliberate and free in saying "yes" to God's plans for me. In silence I allow myself to be the vehicle for his word, by trying to live it first and then communicating it to others.

In silence I can write more effectively, think with greater clarity, relax, do nothing, be. For me, silence is not empty. It is fullness. Silence is my treat.

Can you afford to take a one-minute vacation from whatever you happen to be doing right now? Shut down every sound and noise around you, and enter the temple of silence, alone. Try it.

What did you feel? Were you comfortable, relaxed, happy, or were you nervous, anxious, scared? How many times did you look at your watch? When you begin to get accustomed to silence, it will no longer be an "unusual" experience.

Silence is the appropriate climate for spiritual life. It is true, of course, that God is present in our lives at anytime, but we are more likely to feel his presence in a more decisive and intimate way when we seek out silence. The prayer that then emerges from that silence is called contemplative prayer.

In contemplative prayer, perhaps the highest form of prayer, we focus totally on the present reality of God. We choose not only our silent surroundings, by shutting down all noises, but also the silence of the mind and heart, by concentrating all our attention and desires on God alone. We also enter the silence of the will, by wanting only what God wants.

This prayer silence—contemplative prayer—is more than a simple act, however; it is a process of becoming. We willfully stop any foreign distraction to concentrate on our union with God. There, in full and true silence, only this

The Prayer Silence

loving union with God remains. The process becomes a
state of being.

Silence is not just an empty space and an empty time.
It is not a scary void. Notice, for example, how in an empty
room, we often realize more light, more fresh air, greater
space. In a similar way, true silence is the fullness of more.
The distractions and noises that fill our hectic modern lives
make us hungry, impatient, anxious, and worried. By losing
silence, we lose the opportunity of allowing more room for
God's fullness to enter our lives.

Only through the prayer silence can we find what we
cannot find elsewhere. In silence we find that "there is need
of only one thing" (Luke 10:42).

✙

Individual prayer opens our personal lives to God. Praying with others, however, draws separate lives together into a new unity: a community of being. Praying with others allows us to witness to the unity of the members of the Church, to our belonging together, to our participation in the mystical Body of Christ, and to the continuing presence of God in the world.

Notice how life offers us all kinds of support groups. People of the same concerns and interests gather together to discuss their favorite concerns and to determine what they can do about those concerns. They share genuinely what they have in common. In a similar fashion, committed Christians need to come together to share their faith, and prayer in common is an expression of a shared faith.

"Going to church" to share with others the same faith is an important part of our faith journey. Churchgoing, however, can become a matter of routine, a habit or, even worse, the fulfillment of a certain "obligation."

Let us think about this for a moment. Ask yourself: "Why do I go to church?" What are your real motivations? Do you go because of a certain social pressure that seems to favor churchgoing? Because the church is a good and safe place to meet others? Because everyone in the family is going? Because if you don't go, you commit a sin? Because the chanting is beautiful, the sermon is captivating, or the ritual is nice? Because you like that particular priest? You can, no doubt, find many other reasons for attending church celebrations.

But have you thought about going to church for the purpose of joining others of the same faith, those who belong to the same church, to pray together and thus demonstrate concretely that "we" are one Body and that our prayers are heard by the same God?

When we genuinely pray together, we experience ourselves as a more unified, more loving community. Mother Teresa of Calcutta would have said that praying together means the willingness to stay together. Thus when we worship together, we join as active participants not just "spectators."

Shared worship usually takes the form of structured prayer—rites, gestures, and readings established in advance— that is usually directed by a "leader." Those gathered for this shared worship join their voices and gestures to what is already there; to sing, read, and offer prayers and responses together. They join their intentions to the intentions of everyone else gathered, thus becoming one with them. The community remembers all those who have died and those who cannot be present with them at this particular time. As a community, people pray for those they like and those they don't like—always remembering that all are members of the one Body.

Praying with a community of believers is a way in which the Holy Spirit feeds us, nurtures us, and helps us unify and grow closer to one another—whether we worship in a great cathedral among thousands of people with beautiful music and words, or in a small quiet room with two or three persons who can share everyday words. For "where two or three are gathered in my name, I am there among them" (Matthew 18:20). In either case, the Holy Spirit can make of us a new creation by transforming us from the many into the one Body of Christ. Coming together in prayer continues Christ's earthly incarnation, and his touch empowers us to do things we could never do before. The Holy Spirit becomes our wings in the world.

Because we gather in faith and love to share God's love, praying together is an essential part of our Christian life.

It is amazing to see how bodily peace can help us reach mental peace, emotional peace, and spiritual peace.

The body is far more important than what we have learned from Western theology and spirituality—influenced by Greek philosophy which separated body and spirit. In the duelist system, there are two entities: spirit and matter, soul and body. Spirit is good; matter is evil. Therefore body is bad.

Seneca spoke of the detestable habitation of the body; Plato described the body as the prison house of the soul, saying that only the spirit matters. Docetism didn't want to admit that Jesus had a real body. Augustinism, which was heavily characterized by this kind of dualism, left an immense impact on Christian spirituality, believing that the soul must tame, suppress, and control the body, for the body is an obstacle to holiness.

No wonder this way of thinking can lead to a "holy" hatred of the body, to flagellations, and self-hurting. To some hermits, a filthy body was actually a virtue. Thank God we no longer think this way—although we may have in the back of our minds some remaining scars of that dualistic point of view.

We cannot live our faith as if the Incarnation did not occur. A Christianity that does not celebrate in action "the Word made flesh" is not the Christianity of Jesus Christ. In the Incarnation, the walls of hostility, division, and fragmentation between all that is have collapsed, giving way to reconciliation and integrative and redemptive love. Saint Paul cannot help but say, "Do you not know that your body is a temple of the Holy Spirit within you?" (1 Corinthians 6:19)—and we must treat our body as we treat a temple. The kingdom of heaven is within! In our bodies, our personal stories are written, the mysteries of our lives are unveiled, and the exit for our abstractions is found.

Nowadays, when we talk about illness, we often speak of psychosomatic illness, and when we talk about healing, we speak of holistic well-being. I am a total body-spirit person. We live and move in and through the infinite love of the Holy Spirit. Because there is an intimate connection between bodily health and spiritual energy, it is important for us to develop a praying body. Change your body by changing your state of mind; change your state of mind by changing your body. Today modern scientists see the physical and the spiritual as different expressions of the same order.

When we were young, we learned that prayer is the raising of the mind and the heart to God. At that time, this was a beautiful definition of prayer. Yet, this definition is culturally conditioned. Indeed, it was a good definition for an age that idealized the mind and the heart while considering the body to be a "burden," a "prison," evil. But that age is gone. Today we are discovering enormous potential and mysterious energies in the human body. We are learning more about vibrations, auras, alpha waves, energy fields, acupuncture, body language, and psychic powers. We especially know more about the role of the body chemistry in our emotional, mental, and religious life. We know, for example, that the personality can be changed by chemical addiction, and that depression, anger, and anxiety can be attributed to adrenaline or melatonin or hormones in our bodies. We also know that depression can be related to nutrition. We know how important breathing is: Good breathing can bring tranquillity and bad breathing can increase distress. We know how important diet and exercise are: We are what we eat and drink, and we are how we exercise.

Our approach to prayer is affected by all these things because prayer is an activity of the whole person. We do not raise to God our mind and heart alone, but our entire being: our thoughts, feelings, breathing, head, hands, feet, blood, bones. In prayer, we hold nothing back from God. After all, our body is not bad. The Lord became flesh as we are flesh. He is in every atom of our body, and thus we love him with our entire being: body and soul.

So, just as organs, guitars, incense, and stained-glass windows may create an atmosphere in which we find ourselves drawn to prayer, we want to make sure to train our bodies in a lifestyle that will make prayer easier to achieve. For example, watch your diet, learn how to breathe, learn body-awareness, learn to be still and to quiet yourself, exercise, take up some sports to stay in good shape, walk as much as you can, adopt a healthy posture, and always see your body as a temple—for, indeed, it is the temple of the Holy Spirit (see 1 Corinthians 6:19).

Pray with all your being—including your body. Hold nothing back from God. Pray with all your humanness.

Develop a Praying Body

Who needs saints today? This is a fair question, isn't it?

Somehow, when we think about saints, our imaginations go back in time and we picture extraordinary people like Paul, Basil, Benedict, Augustine, Bernard, Francis, and Thérèse. We find ourselves wondering what these people can say to us today, in a world of computers, competition, business, sex, violence, and the almighty dollar. Who listens to the saints today?

Actually, if we listen to the saints today, we hear them say that ordinary lives, like yours and mine, are the ingredients for sanctity. Just a simple, loving, prayerful life makes a difference, not only at the personal level but in the whole world.

Is this true? What is the saints' secret?

Saint Thérèse of Lisieux discovered a "shortcut" to sanctity. She realized that sanctity consists in allowing God to work in us, rather than counting on human efforts and success, even spiritual success. To count totally on the Lord was Thérèse's way of "spiritual childhood," her path of sanctity. Even though she was eager to do great things for Christ, greatness for her did not lie in external achievements but in becoming like a child and surrendering herself unconditionally to God's love. Thérèse died young, at the age of twenty-four. Although she lived in ordinary, humble circumstances, she had a genuine experience of God—and this is what real prayer is. This is what sanctity is. There is no better prayer than experiencing God, and this is the "shortcut" humans can walk to reach sanctity.

Saints appear to be very ordinary, like Thérèse. Because saints are human, we cannot expect perfection in every detail of their lives; saints know failure. But what makes them different is the fact that they are focused, centered, and prayerfully open to the presence of God. Coming from their hearts and voices, we hear the psalmist's words: "Whom have I in heaven but you? And there is nothing on earth that I desire other than you. My flesh and my heart may fail, but God is the strength of my heart and my portion forever" (Psalm 73:25–26).

Saints count on prayer above all else; they know they cannot make it alone. They pray. They know they cannot, by themselves, heal their own wounds or the wounds of others. They pray. They know they can fail at every turn. They pray. They long to be in continuous communion with God. They pray. Saints live ordinary lives but somehow, because of prayer, their ordinary lives become extraordinary: radiant, sparkling, shining with divine flavor. Their union with God transforms their daily activities into meaningful and joyful works. As ordinary people who live extraordinary lives, they contribute to the coming of the kingdom here on earth.

We need saints today. We need them more than we need advanced technologies, eloquent preachers, brilliant minds, and canny politicians.

Abraham, a friend of mine who died a few years ago, was not extraordinary. He wasn't a leader and he wasn't the most intelligent student in class. However, no one could compete with Abraham in the goodness and compassion he showed toward everyone. He lived compassion and was in visible communion with his God. A man of prayer, Abraham lived a

Can We Have Saints Today?

"spiritual childhood." He was real and, by his example, he made a difference in the lives of so many people.

Without God's help through prayer we will not become what we ought to be or what we long to be. Through prayer we may not actually reach sanctity, but we will be on the road—and this is what our world needs most, people of prayer whose lives are living examples of holiness.

We have saints today; *we* are called to be saints today. With their prayers, saints will save our world.

✛

It may take a lifetime to learn the value of this instant—this moment and this place in which we are living right now. It is easy to talk about this moment, but it is hard to put the reality of it into practice.

Both the past and the future are heavy burdens on our shoulders. The image of what and who we have been and the image of what and who we would like to be condition our approaches to life and dictate our behaviors. Because we usually tend to be someone or something we are not, we miss the essence of what we really are. We live in daydreams and miss the present. We live others' lives, not our own. In a sense, we are "secondhand" people living a ghostly existence. There is no originality or uniqueness about us. A copy machine could easily be a symbol of our daily life. We live as slaves in our lifestyles, and we do not know it.

This is not the way our lives are supposed to be lived, however.

We are supposed to prepare the way of the Lord by living "the sacrament of the present moment." This means that we should trust the providence of God's will and live with a filial and total dependence upon God's loving care. The sacrament of the present moment means that, in the twilight of our prayer, in those quiet moments of our intimacy with God, we dare to ask questions such as: "Lord, who do you say I am? Am I really me? Am I really your child? Am I trusting you as your child, totally?"

To be worried, anxious, and afraid is not a Christian attitude. Rather, a Christian should have only a deeply optimistic vision, as only faith can direct it to be. In a social order that is increasingly marked by aggression, mistrust, self-defense, isolation, and a search for personal gain and egotistic fulfillment, a genuine spiritual "letting go" is the Christian's orientation. Why are we afraid? "Take heart, it is I; do not be afraid" (Matthew 14:27). "Look at the birds of the air; they neither sow nor reap nor gather into barns, and yet your heavenly Father feeds them. Are you not of more value than they?" (Matthew 6:26) "Take nothing for your journey, no staff nor bag, nor bread, nor money—not even an extra tunic" (Luke 9:3). Is what Jesus asking of us possible to carry out at the human level? Is this real?

The Lord is asking us to travel light and free. He wants us to know that nothing is more important than him. When we realize this, we will not have the need to escape to the so-called freedoms, for we will know that real freedom is within.

Jesus is saying more than "Do not take a bunch of material things on the journey," for there are other things, visible and invisible, that can burden our journey of faith. Frustrations, despairs, pains, hidden angers and motivations, worries, dishonest ways and patterns, and those inner voices that tell us to be perfect, do the most, be the best, be competitive, win: All these things are burdens that weigh us down, that make us too "heavy" for the journey, that prevent us from being able to relax, play, celebrate, sing, and be ecstatic. As Christians we are to surrender the weight of our load to the One who said: "Come to me, all you who are weary and

"The Sacrament of the Present Moment"

are carrying heavy burdens, and I will give you rest" (Matthew 11:28) and "My grace is sufficient for you" (2 Corinthians 12:9).

To live in the present moment is to live with total trust in the providence of God's will, for the present moment is the meeting point between God's will and our reaction. This is why we should live every moment to its fullest, with the maximum amount of loving life.

To live in the present moment means to experience the sacredness of each moment by living it in full consciousness and being completely involved with what we are doing. This is an ecstatic identification with the unique moment, for all our energies become fully merged with and in the present. We become the moment, completely open to the Holy Spirit, whole, aware, filled with his divine grace.

At this level of understanding and depth of living, everything we touch will turn to prayer and, somehow, our prayer will seize us with a passion for connection with everything. Through prayer, our perceptions and consciousness are radically altered.

To live the present moment prayerfully is to find what we cannot find elsewhere: the peace that is not of this world, the bounty of a healthy life, and the unending joy that only God can give. In the sacrament of the present moment we have real life, and we have it abundantly.

⁜

If we are to pray effectively and confidently, we must pick the right place to pray. A well-selected place for prayer helps us pray better, with greater depth.

Across the street from where I lived in Paris there was an old church. I loved that church. Can you imagine how many people have prayed in that church over the past three hundred years! That church has a silent, peaceful atmosphere about it that would make me feel like I was in communion with God and all who have prayed there before me. I also liked to go to Notre-Dame de Paris and the Sacré-Coeur de Montmartre, especially for major solemnities. These great churches are truly inspiring. However, there were times when I found my inspiration for prayer in the nearby park, le Jardin du Luxembourg.

A church can be a favorite place for prayer, but we must not be duped. If God is not in our heart in the first place, we are not going to find him in a building called a "church."

Another good place for prayer is a seldom-used room in your home: "Go into your room and shut the door and pray to your Father who is in secret" (Matthew 6:6). Perhaps you can pray in your bedroom, your office, the garage. You can pray frequently in your living room; always in your dining room; definitely in your car. Why not under the tree in your backyard? Why not anywhere? God listens to you anywhere, anytime. Be assured of that reality. God always has time for you, for you are his child. You can knock at his door from anyplace you want, and he will be there. He welcomes your morning prayer, your noon and supper-time prayer, your prayer immediately before retiring. Just relax your body, take a deep breath, close your eyes, say what you want to say to the Lord, and listen to your heartbeat and to what the Lord says to you.

A private place for prayer has many advantages. For example, it allows you a comfortable freedom for expressing yourself—in the event you want to sit perfectly still, lift your arms upward, cry, smile, utter things out loud, or be silent. A private place allows you to use your freedom and spontaneity in prayer—and God loves spontaneity and unconventional things just as much as he loves ritual and programmed words. God is creativity.

There is something very special about the outdoors, too, that attracts not only artists and poets but worshipers as well. Nature has special "vibrations." Indeed, a beautiful sunrise or sunset, moonlight shining brightly through the trees, twinkling stars on a clear night, the quiet trickle of a river, a peaceful mountaintop overlooking a crystalline lake, an inviting seashore with the sound of waves lapping on the sand: These elements of nature can affect the quality of your prayer. Jesus, our master in the art of prayer, did it before us: "He went up on the mountain by himself to pray" (Matthew 14:23). "He went up on the mountain to pray" (Mark 6:46). "He went out to the mountain to pray; and he spent the night in prayer to God" (Luke 6:12). "Jesus took Peter, John and James, and went up onto a mountain to pray" (Luke 9:28). Learn also from the psalmist, Isaiah, Francis of Assisi, and John of the Cross. Learn from the mystics, who traveled to

Prayer Places

mountains and deserts to find suitable sacred places for their prayers and meditations. Even if you're in a downtown area, a busy marketplace, or a crowded location, try to find a secluded place of natural beauty for your prayer. Spiritual masters think that nature helps people pray, sometimes in substantially good ways. Besides the church I go to and the little quiet place in my home, my favorite temple for prayer is nature. I pray while walking in a park—and somehow autumn is the most inspiring season of prayer to me.

Pray there and here, anywhere, anytime. You can commune with God in St. Peter's Basilica, in the kitchen, in the subway, in the bustle of Fifth Avenue, by the bank of a stream, or under a tree. Pray wherever you feel closest to the Lord. Find whatever works best for you at that particular moment in your life. Let Mother Nature teach you to be, which is exactly what we all need in this world of frenetic activity. To be in the presence of the Lord is the very essence of prayer—and we can be in his presence anywhere and anytime. In fact, we are.

✥

The following questions will help you reflect on what you've read. Give yourself some time to ponder these questions attentively. You may want to answer these questions with a kindred spirit or a small faith community or, if you prefer, in the quiet of your room, heart, and mind. Whatever your approach, be honest, direct, and straightforward with yourself. Do not compare your answers with others' answers; competition is not allowed, nor is scoring points of any concern. Just be yourself. You will see what a difference it makes.

As you reflect on these questions, leave yourself open to similar questions that may come to mind.

1.   What does prayer mean to me?
2.   When do I pray? (In times of troubles? When I am happy? When I am in need? Anytime?)
3.   At what time of the day or night do I pray?
4.   How do I pray? (Do I use a prayer book? Do I recite prayers I have memorized? Do I pray using my own words? In silence? Just listening?)
5.   Who taught me to pray?
6.   What were my earliest prayers?
7.   Has my prayer changed over the years? If so, how and why?
8.   What does the prayer that I pray tell me about myself?
9.   What does my prayer tell me about the God to whom I pray?
10. Does my prayer help me know God the way God really is, not the way I try to make him look?

11. Do I allow myself to tell God whatever I have in mind and heart? Do I have to pretend to be other than I am? Do I have to fool myself and God? Can I fool myself and God?

12. When I pray, do I talk to God more than I listen?

13. Does my prayer express a certain good feeling I was looking for, or is it an expression of deep faith and trust?

14. Can all of my life be prayer? Why? How? Is "praying without ceasing" (1 Thessalonians 5:17) possible?

15. What are the profound motivations of my prayer? (Duty? Love? Gratitude? Joy? Suffering? Troubles?)

16. What does the God I pray to look like? (Judge? Tyrant? Compassionate? Up there? Down here? Indifferent? Neighborly? Human?)

17. Has my image of God changed over the years? If so, how and why?

18. Do I feel the need to experience God differently?

19. Is God active in my life? Do I let God be involved in all my life or only a part of it? In what part of my life don't I want God to be involved?

20. Is my relationship with God one of a kind? Do I relate to him as I am or as someone else?

21. Am I able to develop a friendship with God in my everyday life? Does God make a difference in my life?

22. What do I like least about my relationship with God?

23. Do my answers to these questions tell me what kind of God I relate to and what kind of person I am?

24. Why should I tell God something he already knows?

Reviewing This Book and Your Life

25. Is prayer a waste of time or is it a time for building up my relationship with God?

26. Does prayer seem a duty to me? Why or why not?

27. Where do I usually find God? Is he in:

- the Bible
- the Church
- Holy Communion
- confession
- chanting
- works of charity
- nature
- music
- art
- books
- study
- challenges
- friendship
- people
- joy
- up there
- here and now
- none of the above
- somewhere else (if so, name where)

28. Do I really want what I pray for, for myself? For others?

29. Do I keep focusing on the same petitions? Why don't I have what I am asking for?

Reviewing This Book and Your Life

30. Who are the persons I've prayed for recently? Did my prayer make a difference in their lives? In my life?

31. Do I usually ask others to pray for me? Do I tell them my specific needs?

32. Do I pray for such things as winning the lottery, getting a promotion, or having good weather next weekend?

33. Do I have a tendency to bargain with God? For example, do I tell God that if I get what I'm praying for, I'll go to Mass every day and light a candle after each Mass?

34. Am I able to identify the people in my life who were instruments of God's presence to me?

35. What do I like and dislike about my prayers?

36. Do I see any changes in my perceptions after a prayer based upon a deep and close relationship with my God?

37. What difference has my prayer made in my own life?

38. What difference did God make in my life this week? This day?

39. Did my prayer have any recent effect on my family life? My workplace? My own circumstances?

40. Was I able to find time each day this past month for prayer (in words or listening to God)? If not, why?

41. What can I concretely do this day to help God's kingdom come into the world? Into a situation? Into another person's life? Into myself?

42. Do I feel any difference between contemplative prayer and action prayer?

43. Do I feel part of the mystical Body of Christ?

Reviewing This Book and Your Life

44. In what ways might the Lord be calling me personally to grow closer to him? What steps am I going to take this week to properly answer my personal call from God?
45. Am I really "me," or am I someone else?
46. Who and what is God for me? Who and what am I for God? What do I truly think of God? What does he think of me?
47. What impact has the past and the future had on me?
48. Do I live the present moment the way I am supposed to live it?
49. How can I best be a "living prayer" in my own world?
50. What am I doing right now?

If, in answering these questions, you discover that you've found "the way, and the truth, and the life" (John 14:6), don't think that this is the end of your journey. For, in fact, this is only the beginning. Bon voyage! It cannot be otherwise.

✠

Reviewing This Book and Your Life

Toward a Definition of Prayer

NOW THAT WE'VE prayed individually and together, told the Lord all that we have in our minds and hearts, reflected on prayer, and asked ourselves questions that have helped us review our lives and our relationship with God, let us try to define all that we have done.

It may seem strange and odd to *end* with an attempt to define prayer, when one usually *starts* with such a definition. It seems like an upside-down attitude—and it really is. Real prayer puts our lives upside down.

God does not need our words or our definitions; he wants our hearts. And we need God, not just some concept of him, but God himself.

Does the formula H_2O quench your thirst? Does the word "fire" burn you? Does the word "peace" make peace in the world? Do we feed ourselves with just the words from a menu? Of course this does not happen. Formulas can never replace the real. This is true with prayer as well. Words of prayer should be expressions of—but never replace—the prayerful heart. The truth of prayer is not a formula. Rather, it is the experience of God right here, right now. Beware of the conceptual idols of God. Live first the reality of God, then "philosophize" about your experience later, if you really want to do that.

Indeed, prayer has different meanings for different people in different cultures and in different times. It depends on *the one who* is praying, *to whom* that person is praying, and *why and how* that person is praying. Every generation has learned to pray uniquely, again and again and again, for each generation has different needs and thus different ways of expressing those needs and desires. The one sure thing, though, is that when we pray, we should not expect to change God's mind. Prayer does not necessarily set things right. It does, however, make us right. It does not change God; it changes us and, in the process, it changes the world. Prayer is not a good speech that we give to God. Rather, prayer is our open listening to God. Prayer is not an external ceremony. Rather, it is a way of living, a lifestyle, an attitude of being prayerful. Prayer is a continuous conversion to a deeper union with God and the world he created. Prayer is a continuous renewal of our lives and the lives of others. Prayer is the work of God within us. It is God's abundant grace that is helping us in the process of divinization.

Prayer is real only when all that we happen to be doing becomes prayer, which is when prayer becomes "unceasing." At that moment we start to relativize the "values" that we have built our lives upon because they begin to appear like fictitious "realities." We then become like little children, full of wonder and renewed attention to all that God has made, and we transform our daily lives into grateful loving living. Prayer is when we let the Unseen Reality become real in us,

Epilogue: Toward a Definition of Prayer

leaving our own ways and patterns—our "treasures"—and looking forward to new dimensions for ourselves and our world.

Prayer is when we live what we utter—"Thy kingdom come"—and make it happen here and now. At that point, we are holy people, fully human, fully divine, fully alive. It is then that we become "living prayer," "unceasing prayer," and this is the most intimate experience of God possible. God's infinity becomes the very horizon of our lives.

God wants us to have right and prayerful hearts, whether or not we are able to recite the right words and follow the right formulas. Prayerful hearts! This is what prayer is all about.

✛

Epilogue: Toward a Definition of Prayer

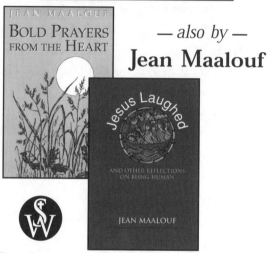